Melvin's Life Story

His Life and Legacy

By

Melvin Siggelkow

Order this book online at www.trafford.com
or email orders@trafford.com

Most Trafford titles are also available at major online book retailers.

Print information available on the last page.

ISBN: 978-1-4251-8993-8 (sc)

Trafford rev. 03/27/2019

www.trafford.com
North America & international
toll-free: 1 888 232 4444 (USA & Canada)
fax: 812 355 4082

Contents

CONTENTS 3

PREFACE 5

FAMILY BACKGROUND 9

HOMESTEADING IN SASKATCHEWAN 18

    1914 26
    1915 27
    1916 29
    1917 30

TRAVELING SOUTH 32

    1918-1919 32

HELPING HANK 37

LIFE ON THE CANADIAN PRAIRIE 40

    1920-1927 40

MOVE TO THE STATES 49

    1928 50

THE RICHLAND POOL HALL 53

    1929-1930 56
    1931-1932 61

WORKING IN MINNESOTA 64

    1933 68

RICHLAND AGAIN 70

    1934 71
    1935 74
    1936 75
    1937 79
    1938 79
    1939 79

OREGON 81

1940'S 81

SCOBEY, MONTANA 89

1960's 100

FORT PECK **102**

1970's 105

1990's 112

GERMANY **112**

THE LAST YEARS **118**

APPENDIX 1 .... **125**

MAPS 125

APPENDIX 2 .... **131**

MELVIN'S DESCENDANTS 131

Preface

By: His Daughters

Rosalie ~

I can plainly see us driving down one of the busy streets in Portland. It was evening, and Dad was doing one of his favorite things, singing. I remember him singing a couple songs in particular: "That Silver Haired Daddy of Mine" and "I Want a Girl ....."

Dad always worked hard. During the War (WW II) he not only worked in the store, he worked at the shipyards. He would leave about 2 p.m., I think, and return about 2 a.m. I suppose he worked the 4-12 shift. I know he wanted to transfer closer to home and the union official said something like, "You're lucky you've got this job", or some such rubbish. Do you suppose that was the beginning of Dad's dislike of unions?

This strong work ethic was something he had throughout his life. For example: farming, running his transfer business and the pool hall at the same time.

Dad also loved to visit. It used to make us girls antsy. For instance, coming home from Uncle Bill's or Uncle Walter's we would barely make the customs by six. Then he would stay and talk. Some of us were teenagers then, and wanted to get to Scobey for the 6:30 show. Sometimes we made it and sometimes we didn't!

Then there was the trip to Wisconsin. Mom and Dad picked me up after summer school. We headed to Iowa to visit Mom's brother and two uncles. After that we went to Wisconsin to visit Dad's relatives. The last day we were there we went to another relative's home. The cousin reminded me of Uncle Bill. He was small in stature. His wife was also small, with snow-white hair. She wanted to treat Dad to a genuine German dish. When she served the meal, I bet my mouth fell open in shock. She was explaining how she had the butcher grind the finest sirloin. To this she added seasoning, onion, etc. She shaped it into a mold shaped like a jello mold, and served it with tomato slices. I don't remember what else. Dad and I took a small amount and actually got it down. Oh – Did I say it was RAW? After we left there Mom said she was afraid I'd gag on it. I didn't, somehow. Soon after we left town we came across a hotdog stand. Needless to say, we stopped and got some food.

Also, Dad had a hard time when his teeth were pulled. He really suffered, and lived on soup. He never cared for soup after that.

Corinne ~

My clearest memories of Portland are of living on the acreage at 148th. I remember one day, when we were still living at the site of the market, Dad was going to work on the house we would be moving to. I wanted to go along. Mom said no, so I snuck into the back of Dad's pickup and went anyway. I was in trouble when I got home, but Dad didn't really seem to mind. That's not the only time I tried that trick. As a child I thought I was getting away with something. Looking back from the perspective of a parent, I can't believe Dad didn't know I was there. He played along with me anyway.

Dad loved animals and small children. He'd always take time to stop and pet a dog or cat; and he liked to tease the children. The children weren't always sure what to make of him.

We had a milk cow in Portland, and some chickens. One morning the cow wasn't around and I was worried that she might have escaped from her pasture. Dad said he thought she was just in the woods having a baby, and we needed to leave her be. She'd want to be alone with her baby.

I loved to hear my folks sing. Dad had a good voice even when he was old. We never owned a car when we lived in Portland. Dad would borrow one from a friend once in a while and we would take a Sunday drive. When we were driving beside the river on the old Columbia River Highway, Dad would sing "Old Man River". When we were in the mountains he'd sing "She'll Be Comin' Round the Mountain". Later, when we moved to the prairie, Dad and Mom would sing old songs like, "We'll build a sweet little nest somewhere in the West and let the rest of the world go by".

Dad's philosophy of work, as he went from one activity to another, was that "a change is as good as a rest".

Dad was a staunch Republican. Not quite the party ticket man his brother, Hank was, but close. He didn't give financially to the party. He gave to groups and individual politicians that had the same principles he had. He said that he was sure Mom, an Independent, cancelled out his vote more often than not. Dad didn't think very highly of the labor unions. He thought they and the politicians were joined at the hip.

Mom was always stressing the importance of obtaining a good education. I didn't realize until I read Dad's story that he was right there with her.

6

Melba ~

I remember once, when we had gone to Moorhead, Minnesota to pick up Corinne or Rosalie from college in the spring, we were low on gas between Culbertson and Scobey. We had driven straight through, not stopping to sleep. It's a long lonely stretch of road. It was late and no gas stations were open. I think we were low on money, too. When we came to a hill, Dad would turn the engine off, coast down the hill, and turn the engine back on at the bottom. We got to Scobey at 2 a.m., and I was ever so glad to see our house. I had had visions of being stranded in the middle of nowhere with wild animals surrounding us, and no help in sight.

I remember when Uncle Bill went on a long distance truck haul with Dad. When they got back, Uncle Bill said he'd never go again because Dad never stopped to eat or sleep. Uncle Bill had managed to get hold of a bag of apples, and that's all he'd had to eat for days! When Dad got behind the wheel, hold on, 'cuz it was always non stop! Mom always said if ever he did stop he'd pull over and sleep in the car across the street from a motel.

Karen ~

I was struck by the number of times Dad was way-laid in his journeys by load and truck/car problems. I can recall two others. *April 4, 1952* Mom, myself, Pastor Benson, Mr. and Mrs. C. Veis waiting at the church that evening for Dad. He had truck problems. It was my baptism…

May 25, 1964. No waiting this time. Commencement exercises for the class of '64. (Truthfully, I didn't know he wasn't there until after the fact.) It didn't matter as I know he was thinking of me.

Another road trip to Pat & Harold's…This time, however, it was not Dad who had the problem. Kermit and Audrey had come to visit, driving their new Hudson. Because it had such a low clearance, Dad tried to talk Kermit into taking Uncle Henry's car. Kermit insisted on driving his car and got stuck. We all learned about waiting for someone to come by and pull us out. We were all late for dinner that Sunday.

I recall coming home one summer in the early 1970's. There was Dad with his tractor, "remodeling the house". Seems Mom thought the living room was too long and narrow. He and Johnie cut the floor joists, hooked up the tractor, and added a couple of feet to the width of the room…..He was an industrious man when faced with a problem, would always come up with a solution. As Uncle Bill said, he could do about anything.

Growing up as he described must have been hard at times. It must have also been very eventful. I think maybe he would have been a good companion for Tom Sawyer. He was an intelligent man; he did not spend much time getting a formal education. I think his childhood taught him much more than what a school had to offer. I believe it taught him to be self reliant, a problem solver, a man of conviction, and one to see a task through to the end at all costs. Life's lessons that can not be taught in a classroom.

After he had his heart attack I was visiting him…and when I was leaving the hospital he said, "I love you, Karen. You know I always have." I do not recall him ever saying those words before…He did not need to speak the words. We felt them every day.

Family Background

My dad, Heinrich August Siggelkow, was born in Germany on March 17, 1861. He always said that everybody celebrated his birthday. We know his mother lived to be at least 96 years old. How much longer she lived we don't know as the first war came and we heard no more. My dad's father died in his forties. He was kicked in the head by a horse. He worked on a farm. As a boy, Dad had to help out on the same farm. Once when Dad was herding geese, one goose was giving him some trouble. He threw a rock at it, hit it on the head, and killed it. He told the boss that a rat had killed it. The boss said, "Those darn rats!"

As far as I know, Dad had two brothers, John and Bill. John was the oldest in the family, ten years older than Dad. He was a carriage builder. I guess Dad hardly knew him due to the difference in their ages. John was in the German army during the war between Germany and France (the Franco-Prussian War). He may have been in the army for quite a while. John came to the United States sometime during the late teens (1910's). He settled in the Milwaukee, Wisconsin area where his two sons, Bill and Paul, and a daughter, Anna lived. We tried to get Dad to go down to see him but he wouldn't. He said he really didn't know him. I think it maybe was the shortage of money.

John's son, Bill, was a carpenter. He had four children: Anita, Walter, William and Loretta. Anita married a man by the name of Edward Mueller and had six children, two girls and four boys: Edward, Richard, Roy, Judith, Robert, and Carla. She lived in Milwaukee. One of her daughters married a railroad man. He collected antiques, and was a strong mason and union man. Walter had two girls: Lois and Joyce. William had two boys: James and William Jr. Loretta married Frank Corona and had four children: Frank, Arlyn, Coryn and James.

Paul was a wagonsmith by trade. He worked as a blacksmith. He worked for Able Schmit, an appliance maker. He had three children: Gertrude, Henry, and Paula. Gertrude married a preacher and lived in Southern Minnesota. Henry had at least one son, Allen. Paula was my age. One of the girls inherited Annie's house in Crandon, Wisconsin.

Annie married Carl Lymbecker. They had no children. Carl was an electrician. They lived in a logging community in Northern Wisconsin and worked at the mill there in Hiles. Later they moved to Crandon, the county seat. At one time Carl was a janitor at Concordia College in Milwaukee.

The only thing I know about Dad's brother, Bill, is that he didn't like mashed potatoes, but learned to eat them anyway. At that time in Germany, in order to learn a trade, young men were apprenticed to a man who could train them. The family he lived with never put enough food on the table to satisfy a young boy's appetite, so mashed potatoes became Bill's favorite food because they would go down the quickest and he could eat more.

Dad also had some sisters but we don't have any record of them. The papers we had with our records were lost twice. The first time was in a fire in the cook car my oldest brother, Louis, worked in. The second set was lost when my dad, a traveling man, tried to jump a freight train and his bag made the train but he didn't.

Dad occasionally got the roaming fever. A Siggelkow told me once that he thought it was in the Siggelkow blood. With my family I'd almost have to agree. This Siggelkow was trying to find out something of his dad who had left his mother with two small boys. She said it wasn't that she didn't love him; she was just tired of moving. When this man grew up and became a truck driver, he would look in the phone book for Siggelkows whenever he stopped. He hoped to locate his father or possibly some other relatives. He contacted me when we were living in Portland. We kept track of each other for many years, but eventually lost contact.

Dad went into the army when he was about 24 years old. He was in for three years; then he get called back and served another three months before he asked to be let out as he wanted to get married. They said as he was twenty-seven years old they would have to let him go. He married Lena Geirsch in 1888. He was called back to the German army after he moved to the United States, but he paid no attention to it.

Louis Henry was born in Germany October 17, 1888.

My parents left Germany on June 26, 1890. Dad was twenty-nine years old. Mother was twenty-four and Louis was one year and eight months old. They sailed from Hamburg on the ship Dania for New York. I was told that, for some reason, they got off at Boston instead. They went to Chicago where my mother's sister lived. Her husband's last name was Piel, Piehl, Peil or Peihl (pronounced with a long I). I am not sure of the spelling of the name. He sponsored my parents to come to this country, because at that time people needed sponsors. He had a meat market, and it seemed that he drank quite a little. I think he died quite young.

The Piels had five daughters. I can't recall all the names of the men they married as I have mislaid my little red book of the twenties. The oldest married a King. He worked for Swift Meats before going into business for himself. He picked up bones to grind up for lime. Swift Meats threatened to put him out of business so he quit that and went back to work for them. Rose marries Frank Labounty. They had two girls and one boy ten years younger than me. There was an Adam (?) Straus. The other two I don't know. One girl married a doctor. The Piels had one boy. The last time I saw the boy was in 1929. He lived in Wheaton, Illinois, which was then about thirty miles west of Chicago.

My parents stayed in Chicago until about 1894. Once Dad went with his brother-in-law with a horse and wagon to buy some goats. Dad asked him what he was going to do with them goats. He said, "Sh, sh. lambs, not goats.

| William | Henry Sr. | Louis | Lena | Henry Jr. |

Heinrich F. (Hank) was born November 18, 1890

Wilhelm Joseph (Bill) was born September 2, 1892

Frieda was born July 8, 1894

After they left Chicago, my parents spent a little time in Toma, Wisconsin. In 1895 they were in Austin, Minnesota. The census reads: Henry-34, Lena-29, Louis-6, Henry-4, Bill-2, and Frieda-6 months. The Siggelkow Tailor Shop was over Rademacher's Store. They must have stayed in Austin until sometime in 1897. Dad said Frieda was three years old when she died of diphtheria. Dad was very fond of her, and it was one of the saddest things in his life. He said she would come and take him by the finger and lead him to the table.

From Austin the family moved to Waterville, then to Sleepy Eye; and in April, 1900, to homestead in North Dakota. The homestead was located 16 miles east of Kenmare, 9 miles from Norma, and 7 miles from Tolley. Walter, Lydia, and I were all born in North Dakota.

Walter Rudolph was born August 15, 1900

Lydia was born August 20, 1902.

Melvin Emil was born September 20, 1904.

Dad said that one time a strong wind took a washtub off the porch. Louis and Dad tried to catch it. It came down about every six feet so they were able to follow it. They could never catch up with it, and it was getting dark so they had to give up the chase. Louis was getting tired and wanted to set down, but Dad would not let him, as they would go to sleep and freeze to death. They never did find the tub.

Mother hung herself. I guess the prairie life and the shortage of money were too much for her. She is buried east of Kenmare, North Dakota, by a German country church that is now closed down. Now Dad had the housework and a nine-month-old baby to take care of. As I think of it now, I don't suppose he had ever done much, if any, cooking. He did have a big German cookbook.

My dad must have had a hard lonesome life in the time when we were young and he took care of us. No doubt he had never done any cooking or caring for kids, and here he was with a three-year-old girl and a nine-month baby.

As I think back, we never had a cake or cookie at home at any time. Dad had a large cake pan, maybe 14x18 inches. He would fill that with bread dough. Then he would slice apples and lay them close together, and that was our apple cake. I don't remember whether he put some sugar on it or not. When Louis and Amanda got married in 1915, they brought us a piece of their wedding cake which was dished out in small pieces. It was a fruit cake. This is the first time that I can remember having real cake. One time, when I was in my teens, I tried to make some cookies. I couldn't understand what the cookbook meant, and they were a failure. No more cookies.

We had a strange childhood. I don't remember ever kissing or hugging anyone. I hugged my dad once. We were sharing a bed and he asked me in German to give him a hug. I know we had feeling and compassion because when anything sad happened, the tears were there trying to get out, but they were always suppressed.

Things come to mind now that did not seem strange back then. We never got candy. We boys rode horseback, but in all the years my dad was on the farm he never rode a horse. He never rode horseback in his life. He always walked unless he had to haul something. Then he would take a team and wagon. Otherwise he walked sometimes eight or ten miles. I went with him once when I was eight or nine years old, and my little feet got mighty tired by the time we got back. In the wintertime, my brother Walter was around more and would ride by horseback to the store that was six miles away. I don't recall what we used for a sleigh; we may have borrowed one from the neighbor. All of our flour and other heavy items, including an order from

Eaton's in Winnipeg for clothes, we hauled in from Verwood, a town near Willow Bunch, about thirty-five miles from home. We also hauled our wheat to Verwood.

Someone put on a picnic once a year by Fife Lake. Dad would never go, but he would give us a little money so we could attend. It cost fifty cents to go in, and we would get a candy bar. I remember one time we rode double; it was about ten miles. Once, when going to the neighbor's, we were all three on an old gray horse we had. I was on the back and was afraid of sliding off. One time McDonalds had a picnic. They had a hip-roofed barn and had tied ropes in the rafters to make swings. We had a lot of fun.

I got along with Dad all right but sometimes would get a little disgusted with him as he had old country ways of doing things. He would have me walk behind ten feet of harrow pulled by three horses over a seven-acre field. I would have to go around and around to break up the dirt lumps into smaller pieces. For a ten or eleven-year-old, that was hard work in that loose dirt. I got pretty tired.

I sometimes wonder when I did go to school, so much of the time I seemed to be doing something else. One spring I poisoned gophers for Jack Dangerfield. I took my shoes off and got a bawling out from Mrs. Dangerfield, but we always went barefoot until the first bare ground would freeze up. In 1912 I was going to school when there was a heavy frost clear to the top of that tall prairie grass. Boy, it was cold! Then the boys came with a pair of shoes. They were not new, but they sure felt good.

Dad wasn't lazy. He tried to provide for us the best he knew how. He'd go out in the hills to pick berries, come home all tired and thirsty, and make jelly. He always went out and dug the coal for winter and put it in the cellar. We never worried about running out of fuel. Those mines at that time had a water problem, and when it got cold and freezing they had to shut down. People, including Dad, would locate coal laying on top of the ground. If it was near a spring the coal would be good; if it was in a dry area the coal from that place would not burn. The mines were open pit mines and as the digging progressed, the hole would collect water. Later on in the twenties, we had underground mines.

Lydia and Dad never got along well. When Lydia was fourteen and fifteen years old, she'd get mad at Dad and take off. The first time she went to McCutheon's. She traveled twelve or fifteen miles, mostly through hills, to get there. Maybe she got a ride part of the way. They gave her a job for a month or so. Then she wrote me where she was and I rode to see her. When they no longer had a need

14

for her they brought her home. I suppose Dad worried and wondered where she was, but I can't recall him saying anything. It's been a long time. Then she went to a family south of Rockglen for the same reason. I can only recall one more time. She went and stayed with the Melvin Werdal family who lived about one mile north of the border.

One summer Walter wasn't around much, maybe because there wasn't much for him to do and he could earn a little pocket money working out. He was working for some people fourteen miles north of us. In the winter he rode horseback to Scobey, which was another forty-four miles. The reason I remember this was he stopped at home over night. He had gotten quite a few one-pound boxes of dried loganberries for the people he was working for. He had eaten some so he opened them all and dumped them all into a feed sack loose. This way they wouldn't know he had eaten any.

When my parents homesteaded in North Dakota, Louis, a twelve-year-old boy, had to take on much of the farm operation. Dad was never a farmer, and after Mother died, he had the house work and small kids to take care of. Cousin Anna came over from Germany to take care of us children, but when she came I don't know. She was Uncle John's daughter. She was there when I was four or five years old as I can remember her playing Santa Claus. She had a big sheepskin coat turned inside out and said in German, "It's cold out there!" Louis could do just about anything. Somewhere I was told he built the barn in North Dakota, and it was a big one. It runs in my mind that we had twenty-four horses. There was a lean-to on each side, one for machinery and the other for, maybe, cattle. Dad was very proud of it. That was one reason he felt so bad about losing the farm. Some years later I heard him asking one of the boys how the barn was. They said it was falling down and he seemed to feel better then. Louis was pretty much all business. If he had a nickel, it was on the books and was to be paid.

Henry, on the other hand, would hold things in and say nothing, just let it build up. For example, when Lydia was keeping house for him, she made lunches for him to take to the field. She would send him a brick cheese sandwich. He did not like the cheese! He never ate the cheese, just threw it away grumbling that she gave the ham to the preacher and gave him the dried cheese; yet he would not say anything to Lydia. He was a hard worker, but a poor manager and a poor mechanic. In the early sixties, he bought a used John Deere combine with a bent shaft. He could not keep the back sieves from breaking apart. For three years he would work on the combine and get it ready for harvest and get in the field. The first thing he knew he would be fighting broken sieves. I am not a combine operator. That was always his job. But I always believed that where there is a problem there is a solution. I told him there had to be a reason for the sieves always breaking. He finally got a new shaft and had no more trouble after that. I went to town to get the combine shaft for him.

Hank

They did not have one in stock. I called Plentywood. They had one, and would get it in the mail which would arrive in Scobey at noontime that day. I don't know if I went back to the field, but I was in the post office at noon. I had to wait for all the sacks to be emptied. No shaft. I had to do some calling, and finally found it at the Plentywood post office. They had forgotten to load it. I had to go to Plentywood to get it. The point is, Henry was two miles from anywhere with nothing to do most of the day. He had stayed with the combine to take the old shaft out. He wasn't very happy. By the time I got out to the field Henry's thoughts of me maybe weren't so good.

Henry was very shy of cameras. He was also conservative in money matters.

Henry was so hard to understand. In the 1950's, when I took over the pool hall which he had financed, I was looking for a renter so I could close it up. I made a deal with a clothing store for a year lease at three hundred dollars a month rent. The building, located in

Scobey, Montana, where the Four Seasons Floral is currently located, was not as wide as the lot and had to be extended out; and the lessee had some other things he wanted changed. It might have cost seven thousand dollars to make the changes. I was happy with the agreement. In ten years the building would be paid for and we would have a better building. Henry would not go along. It was a plain "no", and no further discussion. I could have gone ahead as the lessee would have advanced the money. But I had no investment. It was Henry's money. We spent five thousand dollars and rented it for five years at $150 a month.

Homesteading in Saskatchewan

The men filed for homesteads near Fife Lake, Saskatchewan, Canada, in 1909. Louis got a nice half section. Dad's was not so good, as it took in some of the alkali lake. Someone had already filed on the piece Dad had picked out, so he did not get it. He filed on a half section about four miles from the others. He started to build a sod house, but discovered that he was doing it on a neighbor's land so he had to pick another spot for his house. The second choice was the better one because it was closer to the road. Then comes Henry with only a quarter section, and some of that in the lake. Maybe he never proved it up (Preemption-file on a quarter section and get another quarter if you live on it for three years and pay six hundred dollars). By my map, the piece of land next to Henry's was not filed on till 1914.

Bill got a half section joining Henry's in 1911. Bill was going on nineteen. With the other boys to do the chores and field work on a half section, he was dishwasher and whatever. I know he did the cooking when Dad was gone. He stayed in North Dakota for a year after we left. He was going to make his fortune selling books. In 1915 he helped cut Dad's wheat, Henry's wheat, and his own wheat. I remember the harvest. It had snowed and the wheat was lying down, so we could only cut one direction. It was my job to keep the horses moving when they pulled the binder back empty. Bill purchased Henry's quarter section when Henry moved to Montana in 1916. Bill herded sheep for Louis Chartrand for four years. Then he went to farming. He got married to Fannie Wagner in February of 1925. In the spring of 1925 Louis Chartrand sold his sheep and went into cattle. Later he wanted to sell out. I said that it looked like a pretty good deal, it was a nice ranch. It was a cold, stormy day. Bill said, "Yes, but if you had that, you'd be out there working instead of sitting by the stove."

Dad and Louis had picked the land out. This I remember because they were gone a long time. While they were picking out the land, Henry and Walter were bringing the steam engine home from Flaxton, North Dakota. Bill was supposed to be watching over Lydia and I, and cooking for us. Henry came and got him to help them with the engine and we were left alone. We went hungry. Henry worked with the man in the firebox to somehow work the flues over to stop them from leaking. There were a lot of flues and it took a long time.

We moved from North Dakota to Saskatchewan just before Christmas in 1910. The first winter, 1910-11, I spent some time with the bachelors around. I stayed with the Dangerfields for a while, then with Henry McLeod. Then I stayed with Henry and William McCraig as they were baching together. Some years later William was at a rodeo picnic laying in the shade under the grandstand when it gave way and killed him.

When we moved over to Dad's place, Lydia and I were left alone pretty much all of the time. There is a hilly area starting about one mile from our house. Dad went in those hills to pick berries; and he mined and hauled our coal for the first seven or eight years, and some of it later on too. He put it in the cellar, which, as with all things, wasn't easy. It was carried by bucket and put down through a trap door, but we always had enough coal for the winter.

The homestead in Saskatchewan; painting by Patricia Siggelkow

The coal mines in those days were surface mines and there was normally a spring which, as they got back farther into the hill and the coal seemed to get deeper, it was hard to get the water out. As the weather got cold and freezing, it meant no coal. One night just as the sun was going down, I saw our neighbor go by. I think it was about twenty degrees below zero. He was going to where Rockglen is now, ten miles or more, so he would be first in line to get some coal in the morning.

There wasn't any wood near our farm so Dad would carry some home for kindling as we had a cook stove and a big heater for heat and cooking. He more than likely carried these pieces of wood three or four miles. Over the years my dad used cow chips in the cook stove. He always had a sack or two on hand in case it rained. They made a fire and would go out so the house never got heated up in the summer. One time Dad took off in the evening and left the bottom door of the stove open. He told us to be careful and not break it off, but some way we did. We were pretty much like the tumbling weeds, done as we pleased and forgot the consequences.

We had a fly problem which went on for many years as there was no spray. Sometimes Dad would hang a bunch of weeds or something near the door for them to gather in and then he would throw it out when it got dark and they were all resting.

We had a chicken hawk problem. They would get the chickens. We had a high pole and put a gopher trap on top of it. When the hawks sat down on it they were in trouble.

We dug shallow wells for water, mostly on a bank next to a coulee. Some people dug deeper wells but there was always the danger of gas. They would put a lighted lantern down the well in the evening. If it was out in the morning, they wouldn't dig any more. Years later my dad had a well dug by a machine. They used two horses to turn it. When he had a witcher come around to find water, the witcher said there was no water near the house. The witcher would walk along and throw down his cap or something to mark the spot where water was located. He said there was water at 150 feet about 700 feet from the buildings. But Dad had to try for water by the house, got down 80 feet, and hit some hard pan. They couldn't get through. They put in a shot of dynamite and the sand above caved in. (I think there might have been water under the hard pan, as there usually is coal underneath it.) Down to the other well site they went, dug down 148 feet and hit water, a good stream for the pump we had then. Dad bought a 1½ horsepower gas engine to pump the water. In my wandering, I stopped by John McIntosh's one day. While talking to him he mentioned that it had frozen pretty hard the night before and some neighbors had forgotten to drain the little pump on the engine and it broke. You guessed it. We had one broke, too. I used a lot of wire and sticks and got so I could keep most of the water in it. Of course this got on to about 1916. My dad bought a windmill from Pete Larson in Scobey to pump the water. Pete marked it as a demonstrator to cut the cost as we had to pay duty on something everyone could see. Some neighbors bought a phonograph in Scobey and smuggled it to Canada. Years later the inspection officers got wind of it, and they either had to give up the phonograph or pay the duty on it. I suppose I smuggled down a load of wheat, but that was different. I had to go about fifty or sixty miles around to get to the customs in order to get home which was only 18 miles away. It was a long cold drive. Of course, by that time I was the man of the farm doing the field work and what-not. When my dad first put me on the one-bottom plow with three horses, I felt big until we hit a rock and that plow sent me to meet another part of it. That iron was hard. But I never got thrown off a plow again. I put the lines in my left hand and held on to the seat with the other, and that stayed with me. Of course, when I got to eight or twelve horses, there were more lines, but the plow was heavier, too.

This is Louis' report of what they did in the first years in Saskatchewan according to a letter he wrote: "In 1911 we (Louis and Henry) moved the breaking outfit (the steam engine they had purchased) from North Dakota to Ogema and broke some prairie in the Bengough area. We moved to Dad's and broke thirty or forty acres, then to McLeod's, then onto the section north of Schmidt's store. Then we broke the strip from the lake to the correction line two and one-half miles on my (Louie's) west line, then ten acres for Dutch, then an eight and one-half acre piece north of my buildings. Then we broke ten acres for Henry and ten acres for Bill. We put up Dad's sod building, made hay, and then went to Weyburn to thresh." Hank (Henry) ran the engine and Louie (Louis) ran the separator.

I can't see how they could do all this in one summer. Even if they shipped the engine part way, they still had over forty miles to get it home. They could only travel about two miles an hour with it. I think they probably didn't begin to break ground until 1912 because they had so much other work to do in establishing the homesteads and getting someplace to live.

Dad's barn was a pretty good size for a sod barn. It held twelve or fourteen horses, two cows, and had a place for the chickens. The chickens were sheltered in a little addition that was constructed of sticks with grass woven between them like it was done in the old country. Dad took some tree limbs or small trees and made a frame. They were set close enough so that he could weave grass through them making a wall tight enough to keep the chickens warm in that cold climate. Then one summer he made a pigpen the same way only he wove tree branches through the framework. This did not work so well as the pigs got their snouts under them and pushed them up. The house wasn't so big as the barn, but it had two foot thick walls and roof.

There was a lot of work to do. They sure must of been busy. In 1912 they broke two hundred acres for McDonald, some for Louis and some for Henry. Somewhere about that time they must have broke seventy or eighty acres for Dad as he had 110 acres broke out on his place. They had several fires. They set fire to a hay stack near Henry's barn, maybe a spark from the engine. Then someone put cylinder oil in the engine boiler and the separator burned one night about 2 a.m. Sabotage by competitors? Dad always figured it was set on fire by competing threshers or whatever.

They had moved a cook car over to Henry's so he could put in his homestead time as you were supposed to live on the land six months every year for three years. One day when he was away the cook car caught fire and burned. Since Louie was handling most of Dad's business and he had the papers in the cook car, most of Dad's business papers all went to smoke, too.

About this time they built a school house four miles away, and we had to walk to school, just in the summer, of course. Late in the fall I still did not have any shoes, and it got pretty cold when the ground got covered with frost. I think I went to school four summers. The first two we walked the four miles and carried our lunch, one egg and one jelly sandwich along with whatever we wanted to drink. There was no water at the school. I never got any more than a fourth grade education, and some in fifth grade.

Miss Jeannne Marit was our teacher and she was a wonderful teacher. She kept us busy and moved us on when possible. She pushed us for all we could do and we learned a lot for the time we had from snow to snow. We could out-spell anyone; and later, Velma said I was a walking calculator. She was there three years, driving seven miles in a buggy. We were sure sorry to see her quit. One time everyone was late for school. I don't remember why, weather maybe. She sent us all home, but we didn't go home. We stopped at the neighbor's and were sliding down the straw stacks and whatever else kids can think of to do. About three in the afternoon she came. Why, I don't know, but she sent us home in a hurry. She invited us up for supper one time in the winter; Lydia, myself, and two neighbor girls. We took the neighbor's sleigh and one of their horses and one of Dad's. As we were eating, one of the girls, Gertrude Jordan, two or three years older than I, saw the moon shining in the window on her back. Some hours later the moon had moved but she thought it should still be on our back going home. It was so bright you could see for miles. I was driving the sleigh. Gertrude kept telling me that we were going the wrong way. I finally turned around to satisfy her, and went to a farm where the road dead-ended. She was satisfied then that I was right and let me turn around and go home.

After Miss Marit left, we got a teacher who was taking up law and took the summer job teaching this school. She had too much night life. She was going out with one of the bachelors and evidently wasn't getting too much sleep and kind of forgot what was going on. She would put her head on the desk and go to sleep. I did not think I was learning too much. I quit going to that school and started riding horseback to the Fife Lake school six miles from home. Lydia was not going at the time. There were two girls, maybe ten and twelve years old, who had to walk seven miles to the first school as they had moved to a small ranch three miles beyond my dad's place.

I found my lack of education to be a handicap in later years. I've gotten along in business doing my bookwork and my tax returns until it got to be too complicated; and then thought that a tax man could save me money. But when I had the pool hall in Richland, Montana I thought it'd be nice to have four barber chairs in there to help with overhead. When I asked at the school, they told me I didn't have enough schooling.

As I have time now to reflect on my life, I recall many things that brought sorrow and joy to my life. Dad never paid much attention to what Lydia and I did. Walter never was around much, either helping Louie or working for someone else. Dad was never a farmer. He wanted to be a horticulturist. His folks said he had to be a tailor, he was too small for anything else. He was about 5'3". Of course at that time the clothes were handmade and there was plenty of work, which changed after the machines came.

One time in the early days my dad had a big rock in the field, and thought the easiest way to get it out of the way was to dig a hole to put it in deeper. Everything went fine. But the rock didn't want to go. So he got down to dig some dirt away and the rock came down on him pinning him in. We went to see why he didn't get home. We got him loose and out, and got the horse and stoneboat and took him home. He came out of it with just a limp through the rest of his life.

About this same time (1912 or 1913) he got sick one spring. I don't know what it was but guess it was serious, as the neighbor came and put mustard plasters on his chest, which we kids had to do from then until he recovered. But through it all we survived. I don't believe I ever had a doctor until I was about 24 years old. For the flu or cold, what they gave you didn't help. You just got over it.

About the third year in Canada, 1913 or 1914, we boys fixed up an old buggy. The turntable was broke. If we turned too far to one side it would stick and we had a job getting it back up. There were a few horses Dad had brought from North Dakota. One was so balky we used her for a saddle horse. Another team was semi-balky and also liked to run away. We took one of the horses to use on the buggy. On our first morning we let him go in a slough to get a drink. When we told him to go he just stood and pawed the water. I don't remember how we got out of there, maybe had to get out in the cold water and lead him out. We could do that. He would stop in the road. We couldn't get him to go. I'd get out, take a line and lead him, get him to trotting, let go, catch the buggy and climb in. If we were lucky, we could get all the way home. Dad had no part in any of this.

Louis and Henry is a sad story. I will give my thoughts for what they might be worth. Louis felt that Henry owed him money. Henry felt he didn't owe any money to Louis. Louis would write letters to Henry asking for the money. Henry never answered them. He would throw a letter down and say to me, "Take care of that." or "You can have that." Maybe I was wrong in not answering Louis' letters for Henry, but I had no answer. They'd have to work it out, which never happened. What a waste over some money that neither one needed. Over the years Henry did not want to talk to Louis. Up until the time he was bedridden and couldn't, Henry would leave whenever Louis came around. This is how it began. Naturally Louis had to be the leader and Henry the gopher. I am sure Henry was holding something in and would not let it out. Maybe in Louis' bookkeeping he allowed himself more wages as he would be the engineer when they were doing the custom farming. I would not think so in a partnership. Henry had four nice horses which they traded for seed. There went Henry's horses. Louis and Dad had horses to start farming. Henry had none. Did Henry get any consideration? I can't help but believe he felt he had been cheated, and locked it in. He sold his wheat and land. He had three thousand dollars when he went to Montana in 1916. He hit three years of no crop. He had his share of bad luck.

Just a few lines on one of Louis' letters to me. He said Dad told him that Henry borrowed eight hundred dollars in 1916 and never paid him. I believe that's true except my understanding of it was that it was four hundred dollars. He also said that Bill owed Dad two thousand dollars since 1920, but Bill never owed Dad any money. Dad sold his land to Bill in 1918. I guess he was pretty discouraged. We had three years with no crop. I think more people left that area at that time than in the thirties. Bill had no money. They took a mortgage on the farm for two thousand. Dad got a thousand and the other thousand was left to be picked up later when Dad needed it. Some people in Florida said there was land to be homesteaded there so we were Florida bound. I wonder if Dad could have homesteaded as he had already homesteaded in North Dakota. There was nothing in Florida, so we went back to Canada. Bill had not been paying on his note, so the deal was off. Bill owed nothing. Dad owed a thousand plus interest which I paid off while I was farming his land. I farmed Dad's land for seven years. I broke 140 acres of prairie. This gave us 250 acres to farm. I think the later homestead years were the happiest time for Dad. It was nice for me, too. While I was farming his land, he did the cooking and took care of the stock. When I was gone he could take off a couple weeks in the summer to prospect for gold, which he liked to do. He spent his winters with me in Richland and then would go back to the farm in the spring. When Velma and I got married he was getting fifteen dollars a month pension. One time when I had the store and he stayed with me, as he was leaving he said, "Looks like you could use a little more stock." He pulled out seventy-five dollars and gave it to me. That would be five months pension.

Louis said that Henry talked him into buying about twenty-five colts together. They built a fence on Henry's land in Montana, and Henry was to keep them until Louis could take them to his place as he had a couple sections of pasture. He never took them. When I came to work for Henry those colts were three-year-old horses. Now some three-year-olds break good and some don't. I bought four of the horses. Three were easy and were good horses although small. The other one...we caught her on a Sunday afternoon, put a harness on her, put her between two quiet horses, and hitched them to a plow. The plow was just to make sure you had control. The next day I drove her on a wagon to my dad's and over to Bill's to help him make hay. I cut hay with her one day. The next morning I went to put a harness on her. She figured that harness meant work and she wanted no more of that. I fought that horse for a couple of hours, started to wreck Bill's barn, give up, took her back to Montana and turned her loose.

In those days, we had a horse fly. They laid their eggs on a horse's lip and as the horse ate hay or whatever, the eggs would work loose and go into the stomach and hatch out worms about, I think, one inch long. If there were enough worms they'd kill a horse. I was at the neighbor's one Sunday afternoon when a big black horse came running from the pasture into the yard and died. They cut it open. It was just full of those worms. We had a kind of wire pill gun about two feet long. You could put a capsule about two inches long into this gun and put it down the horse's throat. Then you pulled the spring and down it went. The medicine would loosen up the worms so that they would pass through the horse. In the early days we'd take some heavy cloth cut in strips so that the horse could flop it around. Then we'd fasten it above the nose. In later years we could buy a wire basket nosebag to put over their nose. The range horses would gather on a hill where there was a little more breeze and the flies wouldn't bother them.

Henry sent me over to a local coal mine to get some coal. The team I had was big horses and one was blind. While waiting to get loaded I turned the horses loose as there was a patch of nice green grass there. The blind horse wandered too far into the soft ground and couldn't get out. He had a good breeching harness on. A neighbor came and we hooked on to the harness with his team thinking this would be enough help to get him out, but he would not budge. Well, I'm getting worried about this time. I was seven miles from home and one horse stuck. I was sixteen years old. A man came along and said, "No problem." He put a log chain on the horse's neck, hitched on and pulled him out. I really thought I'd see a horse minus a head. We used the same method to pull several horses out of bogs in later years with no harm done.

1914

In the summer of 1914 Louis built a house out of lumber for Dad. Then we had a cyclone and hail storm. We kids were in the new house when it hit. It broke out the windows and left deep holes in the siding, but the house did not blow away. We did not know what to do. We went down in the cellar, but the water was coming through the floor. We got out of there and went to the sod house where Dad was. He let us in, and as he opened the door the wind came in and took the roof off. We went down in a kind of pit with planks over it and stayed there till it passed. The storm took our neighbor's shack away and moved another neighbor's new house about six feet. The wind carried some of the metal remains of the separator that had burned in 1912 about a half-mile away from where we had stacked them.

Some of the neighbors were building a road about five miles from there when the storm hit. One said he was laying on the ground hanging on to the grass to keep from blowing away. Another man came rolling along with the wind, so he did the same. Of course the crop was gone, and that was it for that year. We had a dog we were quite attached to, as we had had to shoot our other dog when he got mixed up with a porcupine. One day Walter was cutting some of the grain for feed with a mower. This pup got in the grain in front of the sickle and got two legs cut off. Some more sad kids.

One time, when Walter was staying with Louis, on a cold winter day he talked me into riding back to Louis' place with him. I froze my legs and got a few blisters before they healed. Then Louis had us out shingling his shop. Not so cold that day, though it was still February.

1915
Come 1915 we had a nice crop coming up. Fifteen was a good year for some folks, but our wheat wasn't cut and we had an early snow; so we had to cut it one way with a seven-foot binder. My job was to sit on a seat over the two little wheels in front and whip the horses so they would trot while we were going back empty. When we finished Dad's we went to cut Bill's and Henry's crops.

Louis married Amanda Ruth Boetcher at Northgate, Saskatchewan on February 16, 1915.

Louis & Amanda
Feb.15, 1915

1926, Kenmare, North Dakota
Amanda, Dave, Ernie, Ruth, John, Louise, Louis
Phil hadn't yet been born.

50th anniversary 1965
Seated: Louise, Louie, Amanda, Ernie
Back: Louise's husband, Dan Willford, Ruby & John ; Inez & Phil, Eunice
and Dave, Mary & Ian Lockie, Ernie's wife Clara
Missing: Jack and Ruth Blizzard

Their First Home, a Sod House

One night Bill decided to go to the threshing rig, as Louis and Henry didn't have a house there, so we were camping out pretty much in a granary he had built on his land. At that time the coyotes used to howl at night. These things you don't forget. Louis and Henry pulled the cook car with them when they did their custom work. Louis' wife, Manda, and her sister, Ella, were there cooking for the men. They told Bill off for leaving me alone; but we were left alone a lot, so it seems, and he didn't think too much of leaving me. Bill later came and found a barrel tipped over with me watching the coyotes from behind it.

I don't know what Walter done. Most of the time he was working for some farmers around there. Most of the people at that time didn't have too much land broke, maybe forty or fifty acres or less. Dad had 110 acres which the boys broke for him with the engine. That's all he had until I broke up most of it in the twenties.

1916

In the summer of 1916, Scobey was getting to be quite a town. One morning Henry and I started for Scobey with two loads of wheat. He had four horses, and I had two with a smaller load. It was forty-four miles to Scobey. They had free trade between the U.S. and Canada in those days. The border wasn't patrolled. We were seven miles from home when I started looking for Scobey. We stopped at the Fadness Ranch crossing, which would be about thirteen miles from Scobey, for lunch. By the time we came in sight of Scobey, I had given up ever getting there.

It was the Fourth of July and all rooming houses were full. Henry asked Mr. Scharf if I could sleep in his barn. He said sure, if I didn't mind sleeping on the soft side of a board. I couldn't figure out which side that would be; but the next morning I found myself sleeping on a pile of sacked flour in the elevator. I don't know how I got there.

I don't remember too much till fall. I guess I went to school. Then I had the job of hauling straw for the steam engine. Not too bad, as we could put the rack underneath the blower and fill it up. But I had to unload it. I wasn't that big, and I got so tired I could hardly make it. One time I told Louis I couldn't do it any more. He got mad and bawled me out. One of the men, Art Hanson's brother, took my part and told him to leave me alone, I was played out. Anyway, I finished the fall. Guess I made about thirty dollars. I got a dollar a day.

1917

In 1917 the crop wasn't too good. The dry years were coming on. I was flunky that fall. That is, I had to haul the water for the cooks, take out lunches, and get the vegetables and groceries. The cook wasn't too well liked. She had two pretty teenage daughters helping at different times. She had a time keeping the men away but she managed. Once they decided they would get under the cook car and shake it, as there were some pretty husky men in the crew. The bunkhouse was fastened right behind the cook car, and she heard the plans. She was ready for them. When they got under the cook car, she poured boiling water on the floor. She lived near Hank's homestead in Montana. He drove them to Canada to where the cook car was. One of the girls sat beside him on the ride north, but he was so shy he wouldn't talk. The girl said that he was so busy trying to keep the car on the road that he didn't have time to talk. Enough of that!

Hank had two accidents that summer. He ran into a hole and broke the axle to the engine. Then, at threshing time, a pipe on the steam engine broke and scalded him. He was badly burned. He went back to Montana quite sick and feverish. A neighbor, Mrs. Henninger, nursed him for a couple of weeks until he recovered.

Nothing too exciting at this time of my life, mostly farm work. Dad didn't do too much field work, and we boys started pretty young to do it ourselves. When I was thirteen years old Hank came up from Montana to Dad's place in Canada to haul Dad's wheat. He hauled it thirty-five miles to Verwood and stayed at my dad's while he was hauling it. It was a slow process and took him about two weeks. I was sent down to his place in Montana to work in the field when it didn't freeze too much. I baked my own bread. The first batch of bread I baked was the best bread I ever baked in my life, just perfect. I bached there by myself. One night I heard loud snoring. I was scared. I couldn't figure it out. The noise seemed to be coming from the floor. If someone had come in to sleep, why would they lay on the floor? I was tired and couldn't do much about it anyway. I finally went to sleep. I woke up in the morning. Nothing there. Then I figured it was one of our horses. He had bad teeth or some problem and made a snoring noise. It was a cold night and they had come up close to the shack to get out of the wind. These shacks were only one board thick, plus a covering of tar paper.

I don't suppose that anyone would believe that I get depressed or sad, but I have; and more so now. As kids, I guess we were no poorer than most and maybe better off than some. We never went hungry or cold. We were bashful and backward. I think I've carried an inferiority complex all my life. I never wanted to work for someone else, afraid I could not do the job right. Yet I have started a business on nothing and it paid out. My brother, Bill, once told me, "You are just like your brother, Louie. You can do anything you put your mind to." As kids, we were pretty much on our own, even to do our own share of the work. Dad never talked to us about the problems of life, just about things that went on with the farm. But we ate our meals together as a family. Now people don't have time. Got to grab a plate and watch TV.

Traveling South
1918-1919

Nineteen-eighteen was another dry year. In the fall Dad sold out to my brother, Bill. Not a smart sale. Bill didn't pay anything down, but they took a $2,000 loan on the land. Dad got $1,000. The other $1,000 remained in the bank to be taken when needed, so we just had a $1,000 mortgage with Holland Loan.

Dad, Lydia and myself took off on the train. Dad had $800 cash and a $200 bank draft, both Canadian. We got to Portal on the border. Dad and I started walking out to Boetcher's place which was twelve miles away. I don't know where Lydia stayed. Maybe at our friends the L.A. Grants. Well, we made it out there and stayed a few days, then went on over to Louis' place at Alameda, Saskatchewan, as he had moved down there in the spring of 1916 or 1917. He had purchased a farm about ten miles from Northgate, at Openshaw which was a depot stop. He wanted to be close to an elevator. He was tired of hauling his grain thirty-five miles.

We stayed a while, then took the train for Florida. We got to Minneapolis. Then we got to Rhinelander, Wisconsin, and they told us we would have to go to another depot a mile away. They told us we could walk across a trestle on the railroad tracks, as there wouldn't be any trains coming. We did this, carrying our bags of belongings as we did not have suitcases. There was a train on the track with its headlight on, as this was late at night. It was hard to believe it wouldn't come at us, but we got safely to the other side. The people there told us we had to go back to the other depot, so back we went with our load.

We got things straightened out and made it to Hiles on a freight train. We had a couple of cousins there, Carl and Annie Lynnbecker. Carl worked in the sawmill and had an eighty-acre homestead. They had a small house and a summer kitchen. Lydia slept on the floor in the summer kitchen. Dad and I slept on the floor in the house by the stove. I remember I froze at night, and when they started that wood stove in the morning; boy, it got hot! I helped to cut the wood for the fire so I got to use the wood twice for heat, one time when cutting it and once when it was burned.

My cousin, Paul, had an eighty acre homestead next to Annie's. He had a horse and a sleigh he had made. It was a good sleigh, as his trade in Germany was wagonmaker. After about a week they took us in the cutter to Crandon, Wisconsin, to catch the train. The trip was pretty hard on the horse. It had to pull a heavy load of four or five people in a two-person sleigh. It was in a sweat by the time we got to Crandon.

We stopped in Indianapolis for a day or two. It was Christmas time. The trains were really crowded, with Christmas travelers standing packed in the cars. Somewhere between there and Pensacola, Dad got to talking to a man on the train. We had to make some transfers, and this man told Lydia and I that we had to get on a certain train. I don't know why we kids were to do this without Dad, but we did. What was intended, I wouldn't know. We asked the conductor if we were on the right train, and he told us it was the wrong train and told us where to go. Dad must not have missed us. I remember Dad and this man were on the right train, still visiting. I seem to remember that it did not seem to bother the man too much when we told him off. We got to Pensacola on a bright, clear morning; quite a change for a boy from Canada. Open streetcars. Had to wait for a train, too.

As we were going to West Bay, we had to change trains about midnight. We were hungry, so thought we'd have a hamburger at a stand there. They were fried so hard we had a hard time eating them. They must have been on the stove a long time.

When we got to Panama City we had to take a boat across the bay. It was scary, as we had to jump a couple feet to get on the boat. It took about four hours to get across. We stayed with an old bachelor in West Bay. The water was so close to the top of the ground (about two feet) it was always warm. We went from there to stay with some people on a so-called farm, as they were the ones who got us to go down there. They had put an ad in the paper asking for Christian people to come down there and homestead. Dad was responding to the ad.

It sure was different from home there. Everyone was so poor. They might have a mule and an ox together on a wagon. Pine trees were slashed and cups put under them to catch the turpentine. You had to watch out for alligators. Well, it wasn't what Dad had in mind, and after a few days, we left. We got a ride with a man in a car, who took people for hire. He took us to another town where there was a railroad. We got on a train which burnt wood, and every few miles we would stop and fill up with wood and go on again. We finally got to the main line. It was night, of course, and the depot was about a mile out of town. We had to take the train some time that night. So we bedded down to sleep on the benches in the depot. A man told us that the train we were taking was on the track and we could sleep in it. He took the cushions out of another seat and made us kids a bed.

Boy, that conductor was mad when he came in, but couldn't do much as we were taking the train. I remember we went through Birmingham at midnight on New Year's Eve and all the whistles were blowing.

I guess we got off in Nashville and took a train west. Our first stop was at Marked Tree, Arkansas. Dad and I walked out in the country about six miles. Rich land there at that time, mostly cotton. Dad always found some German people to visit with, and he found some here. It was a nice farm, but they didn't keep any livestock – no pigs or anything. It was low land and would flood over. We visited for some time and then went back to town.

Next we went to a town about one hundred miles east of Little Rock. Dad made a deal for eighty acres of land with a house on it that was partly built. There were some pretty deep washes along the road that Dad couldn't figure out. The owner of the land lived in Little Rock, so we had to wait a few days before we could talk to him. We stayed with some people there. They were shelling peas. It started to rain, and it rained for three days. The water was two feet deep in places. That was enough for Dad. We had to walk on piles of ties along the railroad track to get to the depot. We were gone again, back to Memphis.

We stopped in Memphis to get work, as money was getting short. It seemed Lydia could get a job, housework I suppose; but Dad was a tailor and there was nothing much for him to do. There was less work for myself. On to Nashville. The track was out, so they took us to Louisville and back down to Nashville. Dumb us, we could of just as well got off in Louisville and saved about ten dollars in fare, as we went there right away, anyway.

Out of money now. We talked to a Travelers' Aid and she suggested the Salvation Army for us kids, and that Dad find a job. He still had the $200 Canadian cashier's check, but it was hard to cash. He found one banker who would cash it for twenty percent discount. Dad wouldn't go for that, so we stayed. He got a job in a tailor shop. I went to work for the Salvation Army. I got $1.95 a week plus room and board. I had my own room. We collected paper, furniture, clothing, and what have you. We didn't do any soliciting, just picked it up when people called in and said they had something to give. We drove one horse on a kind of delivery wagon. My job was to hold the horse and to help load the wagon. Sometimes our work would take us out so that we would not be able to be back in time for lunch. The Salvation Army would give us a quarter or so for lunch. We'd go in a bar and get a bowl of bean soup and save most or part of the lunch money. Of course some of the food the Army served was so-called day old, but I thought it was good. A fifteen-year-old boy can eat, I guess. I don't know much about what Lydia did. She stayed at another post of the Salvation Army for women.

Once it rained a freezing rain for three or four days. The ice got deep on the street and sidewalk. We had a five to ten pound weight we used to lay on the ground to hold the horse while we were loading. Well, he took off with that weight on the ice. It skidded right along, and he did about $300 worth of property damage before he got stopped.

The papers we picked up we would sort into different grades, and bale. When we got a carload we would ship them out. It kind of hurt me that people would have magazines and papers done up real nice, figuring they were to be given to others, and they all went into the press.

We stayed in Louisville about two months. Then, in March, 1919, we took off for Chicago. To save money, Dad thought he and myself could stay at the Salvation Army there, as they were only charging fifty cents a night to sleep. They did not like to have us stay as this was a regular flophouse, beds all over the floor. It was just meant to be a place for bums to spend the night. One night there and we got a couple of rooms on Adam Street for five dollars a week, I think.

I got a job at the National Tea Company packing eggs. Lydia got a job at a tag factory; and of course, Dad went back to tailoring. He did not care for this job as he had always made suits, and now he was mostly just altering. Dad stayed on for a while, maybe a couple of months, then left for Fife Lake again. Lydia and I stayed longer. I was going on fifteen years old. Our cousin, Frank Labounty, said we could not stay by ourselves, and had us stay with them out by Irvin Park. People would come out to the park on Sundays and pick dandelions to make wine.

Dad went back to the farm and tried to farm it with some old machinery. He was not too good with horses. He never rode a horse and walked wherever he went. He had to walk seven miles to get his mail. He was alone for two years until I went back to farm the place.

Lydia and I stayed in Chicago until the first of June, then took a train for Portal, North Dakota. We wanted to go to Boetcher's farm. They lived about two miles north of Northgate which is on the US-Canadian border. At that time the border was open, but the countries were still concerned about people crossing the border. They were not wanting just anybody to come into their country. Some way we convinced those asking us that we were not going to Canada, and got a man to drive us out there. I remember him saying, "I thought so," meaning he knew we were going to Canada. We stayed a few days with the Boetchers. Then they took us to Louis' at Alameda, Saskatchewan. I helped there on the farm and Lydia got a job near Frobisher on a farm. They had a bad storm through there later. The woman and baby were killed and Lydia was in bad shape for a while. We didn't know if she would live, but she finally came out of it. She was brought to Louis' and was in bed there a long time.

About harvest time we went back to Boetcher's, and Mr. Boetcher took us to Flaxton where we caught the train to Whitetail, Montana. There was no public transportation from Whitetail to Scobey and it cost us ten dollars to get a man to take us there in his car. Lydia got a job at the Cozy Café, run by some people by the name of Crawford.

Helping Hank

I started out for Henry's place, got out a ways and caught a ride as far as the nine-mile hill on French Lane. The road had been changed, but I didn't know this. A new grade had been put in about a mile north of the old road. It was dark and I followed the old road through the pasture and got to Henry's about ten at night. As I was walking I could see the lights of cars on the new road, so I know I could have gotten more lifts if I had been on the road.

I stayed with Henry the fall and winter of 1919-20 and on through the summer of 1920. I started working for Henry, and helped him through harvest. That fall the grain was wet because of rain. We spread it out on the floor of a shed, but it still heated up. He sold it to a man who had a butcher shop in Scobey. Then, when winter came along, we dug coal all winter. Henry wanted to find coal for the steam engine, and we went back in the hill about one hundred feet or more on a neighbor's (Olie Amundson) land. There wasn't a month when it didn't warm up enough to start that steam engine and try the coal. It never was any good. There was no moisture in that ground.

In the spring of 1920 we broke up some land at Henry's. Henry ran the engine pulling a disc and did the firing. He's stop, shovel in the coal, and go again. I had six horses on a thing we used to level the sod. It was made out of 2x12's lapped over one another, built so they were a little higher on the front side. You stood on it and drove the horse. It was weighted down with rocks. The plank I was standing on broke loose and went under. My legs went under, too. I was hanging there. Henry was coming towards me and could not see me. I was near the edge of the field. There would not be more than two feet between the engine and the horses. The horses were standing still at that moment, but I knew the noise of the engine would spook them as it came close. I thought my time had come. I managed to break loose a piece of wood that was holding the rocks on, and rolled some of the rocks off. With a stick of wood, I managed to pry the boards apart enough so that I could pull my feet out.

We seeded that hundred and some acres to flax. This was to be my pay for the year, but those grasshoppers just love to chew those flax boles off. Despite the mixture of bran, arsenic, and molasses we spread out in the field by hand, the grasshoppers took all the flax. So went the year.

We had an eight-foot push binder for harvesting the grain. It was pushed by a big pipe with three horses on each side. The driver stood on a platform over a steel wheel connected to a board which was between his legs. This board is what was used to steer the binder. The binder was nice on soft and smooth ground, but it sure kept you awake on new sod! Beulah Ralston drove the horses. The grain was too short to cut and tie, so my job was to keep it away from the elevator, and when we had a load, I'd unload the grain into a stack.

We broke a hanger on the steam engine. The wheels were four feet across. The pin holding it on was one and a half inches wide, eight or nine inches long, and rusted in. I had to get in there and chisel that pin out. It took me a week. We pulled the wheel and had the hanger welded, put it back together; and the hanger broke without even moving the engine. All that work for nothing. But that's farming. On with the story. Henry bought another steam engine like the one we tried to fix, one the bank had taken from someone. He had a man get the separator ready. He had me on the water tank to haul the water for the engine. Those engines only went about two miles an hour. It took us all night to move the engine to Butte Creek, north of Peerless, where we were to start threshing. When we stopped for a break in the morning, one of the men made coffee. I think he put a quart of coffee in a gallon can. Boy, was it strong! But it tasted good after working all night. I stayed with the rig for a week or more; then Henry sent me home to finish the harvest and haul some grain. I was to finish up the fall cutting and whatever else there might be to do. Maybe some of the men thought what I was doing was too much for a sixteen-year-old boy. The harvest crew went from Butte Creek to a place north of Richland to harvest.

When I was at Henry's I had a lantern but no globe. I picked up a piece of flexiglass of some kind and made a globe. It worked good for a couple of nights; and then one night it caught on fire and was gone.

The separator man's boy, who was about my age, was sent to town to get a load of coal. We usually burnt straw in the engine, but I guess during the dry years there wasn't enough. The crops were too short. The boy must have fallen asleep. The horses wandered off the road and he got stuck. Henry sent word to me to get the wagon out and bring it to the rig. By the time I got it out it was getting dark. I did not know where they were threshing, but I finally found them.

At threshing time we had a cook car and bunk car which we pulled behind the separator. The landlord had to feed the horses. This was a bad deal for someone who had only a few acres to thresh. If it happened to rain they might be a week or two getting back into the field; and twenty-eight horses would eat up his whole year's supply of feed he had for his small amount of stock that he needed to farm so few acres. And a lot of the homesteaders didn't seem to get around to getting much land broke.

The men we got for help in those days were no good. All they wanted was a couple days' work and a few good meals and then they were gone, sometimes with a coat or something else they liked. I lost a brand new jacket. It just about kept one person busy hauling men out.

One of the men was caught beating a horse and was fired. The farmer had an eighteen-year-old daughter the old man had taken a shine to. He decided to see her before he left. The farmer beat him back to the house, met him with a shotgun, and told him to keep moving.

There was a young woman doing the cooking. There was a pull-down bed in the cook car, but she decided to sleep in the bunk car with the men. She had a fifteen-year-old girl helping her. The girl followed her to the bunk car and that girl's mother got her home in a hurry.

Water for the steam engine was our problem. There was plenty of water but it had too much alkali in it. We had to find a spring and that was hard to do. Late one afternoon I went down in the hills about ten miles from the threshing rig. I had the water tank and four horses. I got a tank of water and started back. It was getting dark. There was no road, just a trail. On a coulee bank, my water tank tipped over and my horses took off with the wagon. I started walking. The horses went back to the rig and the men came looking for me. I don't remember; I suppose by morning we had the tank back on the wagon and filled with water.

Life on the Canadian Prairie
1920-1927

In the fall of 1920 I went back to Dad in Canada as, by this time, his deal with Bill was all done. I stayed with him seven years. The only difference, we had a thousand dollar mortgage on the farm. I wanted to quit farming with Dad in 1926 as I figured things would change for the worse, but Dad asked me to stay one more year. Dad had some old machinery, a few horses, a couple of cows, and some chickens. Dad farmed on a two-year cycle. He had 110 acres broke. He always had 20 acres in oats. The rest of the land was split into 45 acres of wheat and 45 acres of summer fallow. Most people had only 30 or 40 acres broke, and seeded it year after year, and did not get too much of a crop. I didn't have any money left by the time I got to Dad's, but Dad had flour and sugar, as we always bought a year's supply. So I put in the 1921 crop such as it was. It didn't turn out too good as Dad wasn't a farmer and summer fallowed too late. So it was weedy and had some cutworms. We got by.

When threshing time came I worked for a neighbor who had bought a small threshing outfit. He threshed Dad's. The normal charge was fifteen cents a bushel. They could not thresh ours by the bushel because it was too weedy. The hour charge was ten dollars. That was for four or maybe six men and the outfit. Then Henry moved his outfit up from Montana, and I went and helped him the rest of the fall. For that he gave me a wagon with a 120-bushel tank on it.

We had no radio and not too much to read. There was not much to do in the winter but the chores and to sit by the fire. Henry gave me some old drive belts. I made myself a horse, as I called it. It was a device to mend harness, a kind of vice with a seat on it. You put the leather in the vice, pushed on the clamp, and sewed away. I bought some harness hardware, made some harnesses, and fixed all the harnesses on the place. That kept me busy most of the winter.

The next year, 1922, I guess the crops were better. We had a little more money that year. I bought three horses from Louis for $225 ($75 each). They were some of those we had down to Henry's. I also bought a triple bottom plow. It was something different as it took more horses. I used eight in the spring and twelve in the summer. I borrowed a one-bottom plow from my brother, Bill, and broke up some more sod. Now, because we had more horses, we extended the pasture to 70 acres. I sheeted up the house. It was lathed but had never been plastered, as Dad could not find the right kind of sand. I think I put down a second floor at this time, too. We just had shiplap until then. And times were good in the twenties.

I think that the years I helped Dad on his farm would be the happiest time of his later years. He did the cooking and most of the chores. I took care of the horses. I worked, and when the horses were in the pasture and I was gone, he saw that they had water.

When I first went up to my dad's, my only way to get around was on horseback until the spring of 1925. I bought a buggy at a sale. Then in the spring of 1926 I bought a used Model T Ford. In the fall of 1926 I traded the Ford in on a new Chevrolet coupe. In 1927, no crop and the pool hall not doing too good, I sold out and left Canada.

By 1924 I had all the rest of the land broke up. In the fall of 1926 I was worth $10,000 in property and cash. My feeling at that time was that we had had three good years followed by three poor years, a cycle. It seemed as I was growing, that's the way it was. I told Dad I guessed I'd quit and get out. He said to stay another year. I did. I left the farm in the winter of 1927.

We had a neighbor who farmed with oxen all the years until 1918. He was an old man who lived two or two and a half miles from Dad. We called him Daddy Valens. Another neighbor, a bachelor who lived across the road from us, drove his oxen and farmed both their places. We had a horse which had a bad hoof and would walk slower than the other horses. When one of the oxen got sick they would borrow this horse to finish the work they were doing. Daddy Valens had a little pony he used on a small buggy to get around with. His well was eighty feet deep. He had no pump. He had a small barrel with a hole in the bottom to let the water in. The hole was covered by a flap. The pony

Bill and Fanny at home at Fife Lake

was used to pull the barrel up out of the well. Daddy Valens also bought a team of horses when he sold his oxen. He had never driven any horse. I guess he had a time with them. He came and got me about noon one day to help him bring home some cattle he had in a pasture over at Knox Ranch near where Rockglen is now. It was

Bill and Fanny

getting on to dark by the time we got started back. After we got out a ways, he hollered for me to stop. He was lost and wanted to check the stars. My brother, Bill, lived in that area and I knew the country. I got him home, a little late, but in those days that was nothing unusual.

At this time they came out with an attachment to put on the Model T car. The drive wheels were about 30 inches high and it fastened to the transmission some way. This was supposed to be a small tractor able to pull a two-bottom plow. I don't think there is anyone around who ever saw one, as those Model T's were not made to take that. The attachments went on the scrap pile and probably ended up as bullets during the war.

Bill married Frances (Fannie) Emily Wagner on February 10, 1925 at Little Woody, Saskatchewan. They danced all night. The next day it was my job to take the preacher back to Willow Bunch with a team and sleigh. It was a long day. There was some joke about me marrying Rosie, Fannie's sister; but she was serious. I told her she would have to wait twelve years, as Bill was twelve years older than me. I think she waited twelve years, but finally gave up on me.

Bob Dorothy Gerald
Fanny Bill
1956

42

In 1925 I rented some land in Montana by Henry's. Due to the dry year there was a lot of land laying idle, as people just up and left. I summer fallowed about one hundred twenty acres, using twelve horses on my three-bottom plow. Henry told me he would give me four quiet horses to go with my wild ones. What he gave me were wilder than what I had. One was especially bad. We always put the unruly ones in the middle of the string. These horses were in strings of four. One time I took the harness off and left it right there, and went on with just horse and tugs. We used tugs and hames for harness. They were large and heavy and could just be left in the field with the plow at night.

One day a hailstorm came up. It was not a hard storm and didn't last very long. But with me heading for home with twelve horses and Henry with eight, we had twenty horses and shelter for only eight. All we could do was try to hold them and keep them from running away. We had a mess before we got through. When I started for home, they knew where they were going. I got the first gate open but the next one they went right on through. I couldn't stop them.

Hank and I left Dad's place one morning with two loads of wheat. We went about seven miles, by George Goodie's place. In the coulee, the snow was so deep we were there all day. We left our outfits sitting there and went back to Dad's place. We got going the next morning and got down to Hank's place about ten at night. We had one frozen sandwich. That was all we had and we were hungry. Ralstons were living on Hank's place. They worked for him for a year, but at this time they were just staying in the shack. I guess Mrs. Ralston had never had the experience of being out in the cold all day. She gave us some coffee and cookies. I sure ate a good meal when I got to town the next day.

I had some good crops in the 20's but they had to be hauled thirty-five miles by horses, which at that time, was hard. I had a chance to buy one hundred sixty acres of good level land for $300, but didn't have the money. I had some wheat, I guess, but not time enough to get it hauled out, as a neighbor was looking at the land to buy.

Whenever I crossed the border to farm Dad's land, I just crossed over as we did in those days and never reported through immigration. In later years, I went back and forth through customs when I went to Scobey. At this time, I would go straight north of Hank's to cross. I was an American citizen because I had been born in the United States. But I had property (livestock and equipment) in Canada; and people in that area assumed because my dad was Canadian, I was also Canadian. A man without a country (or a man with two countries).

At this time, as I didn't know how long I might stay in Canada, I thought I'd better cross over legally because I thought I might find myself in trouble if I didn't Only how? I couldn't go through the office after going through more or less as a Canadian. The Canadian customs officer at the Scobey port of entry told me that if he would let me into Canada, the United States officer would not allow me to return to the States. I decided to go to Portal and go legally into Canada by taking the train from there. Louis lived at Northgate at the time, about twelve miles east of Portal and across the line. We took my Model T, Walter, Hank, and myself. We had a lot of flat tires on the way, and blamed it on the tubes, figuring the weather had rotted them. But we had a loose clamp, which went through the rim and pinched the tube. It was about 10 p.m. when we got down to Louie's place (illegally). He told us we would have trouble getting back across the border as it was being patrolled and there was a tower so they could see a long ways. We didn't know the border was being patrolled there. It wasn't being patrolled at Scobey at that time. Walter said, no problem, we could go through Manda's brother's place which was on the border, go a mile south and catch a road into Portal. After spending a couple of days at Louie's, we started back. All went well until we got on the road to Portal. The border patrol stopped us and took us into Portal. After several hours of questioning, they fined us $100 for the car and let us go. Of course this $100 had to be in cash, which we did not have. Up at my Dad's place we had a neighbor who ran an elevator in Portal. He went around and picked up cash here and there. It being Sunday, this was not so easy. He took my check and Henry and Walter were free to go. I still had to get through immigration or else my trip was for nothing. Being picked up didn't help my chances much, but I finally got to take the train to Verwood and back home. Hank talked to our local customs officer at Scobey, and he got $90 back. Not too bad.

In the spring of 1926 I bought a Model T Ford. A neighbor had moved down from Duck Lake, Saskatchewan, and had left two girls up there in the Catholic school. As they had no car, they said if I would go up there and get them, they would pay all expenses. Their boy Cliff went with me. We stopped and got gas at Readlyn, about fifty miles from Moose Jaw. It seemed like a long way, so we thought we should get some gas. We only took a gallon and a half. The man at the station was disgusted. We went on and stopped late at night with some of Cliff's family. The next morning was Sunday. We got up. Everybody was gone to church so we left, and after crossing the Saskatchewan River on the ferry, got to Duck Lake.

Cliff had a sister who lived on a farm a few miles out of Duck Lake. School wasn't out yet, so we would have to wait a few days. We were supposed to stay with her. But.....Cliff was drinking more than he should; and we'd go in the back of these bars. He would buy me a bottle of pop, so if the Mounties came in I would be drinking my pop and all looked okey.

Cliff had a girl friend teaching school up at Meota, north of North Battleford. He found out that there was a dance at Meota and that she would be there, so off we went. It rained and that road was just

Taken about 1932-1933
Mary and Walter with their
two oldest children, Harold
and Orvil. The girls are
Lydia's children, Esther and
Audrey Granes.

Walter

like soapsuds, so we got there just as people were coming out of the dance hall. He found out, or thought he did, where the school was; and nothing would do but we had to go there. We wandered around out there in the hills and found nothing. We got back to Meota and had a flat tire. I told him I'd had it and was going to sleep. I laid down in the back of the car and slept. Cliff got the tire fixed and got gas and was ready to go when I woke up. By this time it was daylight.

We wandered around the hills, but couldn't find the school. Then we met a little girl packing a lunch. Sure enough, that was her school. We asked her to go with us to show us where to go. She said, "No," and headed over through the pasture, which we had to go around. We found the school and there were two girls there. Cliff's girl had an older sister. Cliff and his girl friend took off; and the other girl took over the teaching, as it was still fairly early in the day, and school wasn't out yet. I laid down on the hillside and tried to sleep. It was pretty cold up there. School was almost out for the year. A day or

45

two later we took the two girls and headed back to Duck Lake. We stayed with Cliff's sister on the farm. The girls stayed there, too.

We went to Duck Lake one evening and Cliff and his girl had a misunderstanding or something. He shut our gas line off, figuring that we would go home and leave him, as he was drinking. We didn't leave him. On the way home we had to go through the Indian reservation where they were having a pow wow and dance. Cliff decided to dance with the Indians. He did, but we finally made it back to his sister's home. We had to sleep on the floor, which is where we seemed to have to sleep most of the time. Cliff got up and shut the door hard and wanted me to call the girls and tell them he went to the Indian dance. Why? Who knows. He was drunk. I didn't do it, so he went to sleep.

We got his two sisters, maybe ten and twelve years old, and headed for home. We stopped in Saskatoon and took in the fair. Cliff didn't do anything for the girls to enjoy, so I took it upon myself to see they saw some of the things there. Cliff had run out of money by this time, as I don't suppose his folks figured on liquor. So I was

Joyce   Orvil   Walter   Mary   Don   Harold
Sharon   Rodney

sixteen dollars short when I got home.

Cliff almost got me in trouble. His folks bought a new car that fall, 1926. Some people who had an eating house (they had been following the laying of the railroad tracks) had two daughters. These girls were pretty wild, and only fifteen and seventeen years old. Cliff had planned to take these girls out, and had asked me to go along with him. They were not home, lucky dog. They went out with some other men and the Mounties caught them beyond the law. The man

46

with the seventeen-year-old had to marry her, and the one with the fifteen-year-old got seven lashes.

Walter married Mary Lambert on June 19, 1926.

I bought a brand new car that fall for seven or eight hundred dollars. A Chev coupe.

In the fall of 1926 the railroad came through and I decided to build a pool hall in Constance, near Fife Lake. I talked to the lumberyard owner in Rockglen. I wanted a building twenty-four feet by forty feet. The lumber, he said, would cost me $825. I told him I did not have that much for lumber, so he figured some more and got it down to $535. I paid a man a dollar an hour to build it and set it on rocks as we couldn't buy the lots. The land wasn't plotted out yet. We were just squatters. I bought some pool tables and I was in business.

The people who had the restaurant left in the fall of 1926 to go south for the winter, I guess. I ate at Walter's as it was only ¼ mile from town. In the spring, I bought an oil stove and had a lunch counter for a while until the Chinese came along and opened a restaurant again.

One time four or five of us took a speeder (a hand-pumped railroad car) from the shed at the depot and took it to Fife Lake, the next town, to a dance. During the night the wind came up and we couldn't get the speeder to go against the wind. The wheels just spun on the rails. We had to walk home and walk back the next day to get the speeder.

Winter came on before I got to Rockglen to pay for my lumber. One night Walter took a sleighload of people down to a dance there. The manager of the lumberyard, mistaking Walter for me, cussed him out for not paying his bill. I walked down the next day to pay him. He asked me how I got home from the dance, so I informed him I was the one who owed him the money. Walter and I had a lot of fun in those days, as people would mistake each of us for the other. Once at a dance I met a girl Walter had taken out a few times. I don't think I ever did convince her I was the wrong man.

Winter over, time for farming again. I had wanted to quit farming with Dad in 1926 as I figured things would change, but Dad asked me to stay one more year. I would have gotten out with about $10,000 at that time. I got the crop in and hired a man to summer fallow. Then we got a hailstorm and the crop was gone. I had a sale, but as the others around had gotten hailed too, and another part had frost, there was no money.

Nineteen twenty-seven was a wet summer and roads were few and far between. I covered a lot of miles and got stuck a few times. One time Bill's wife, Fanny, and I went to Rockglen. It's only five miles west of where she and Bill lived, but we could not go down the road that was there. We had to go over the hills to the other side of town and come in from the west. We got stuck twice on that trip and had to get a man with a team to pull us out both times. We got home at ten o'clock that night.

Stuck in the mud

A friend of mine who was involved in the lumberyard in Constance wanted to go to Wood Mountain, as the railroad was coming there. We went to Assiniboia and on to Lafleche and down to Wood Mountain. There was no road across there. About sundown we started for home across country. We followed hills and crossed what we could, going north and east. We finally got to the road at Scout Lake. At 2 a.m. we got home. Never got stuck. Just lucky, I guess. Yes, I traveled lots of miles, for those days, in 1927, and most of it was off road.

I kind of wanted to sell out the pool hall. One day in the fall of 1927 a man came in and said, "I understand you want to sell." Finally after some discussion, we agreed on $1800 cash, I think. The only money I had when I left that area was what I got out of the pool hall.

There was a barber who was working out of the pool hall who figured he would be out of a place to work. He proceeded to get drunk and challenged Bill, the buyer, to a poker game. As a result, I didn't get as much cash, and had to take a note for $800. They had a poker party in the Chinese restaurant that night. One of the men got pretty drunk, so they put him out and locked the door. He picked up an ice cream tub outside, broke a window and said, "I'm coming in." Of course, there wasn't a police officer within twenty miles, so we did the best we knew how. Took him home.

Move to the States

In 1927 we had no crop and the pool hall was not doing too good. I sold out and left Canada. It makes me so sad now to think that I left Dad alone there on the farm. Of course, I had turned the farming over to Walter, and it was his job to see Dad had what he needed. But he was five miles away, not like me living there. Dad used to spend the winters with me when I was in Richland, Montana, but I was gone to Minnesota a couple years. He stayed with me when I came back and started the store. In the summer time he stayed on his farm. Later Walter moved some buildings and made a place for him to live. When Velma and I got married he was alone again; and due to changing laws, I could not go up to see him. In the thirties the immigration laws were changed so that if your parents were naturalized Canadians, you were automatically Canadian. So, if I were to enter Canada, the United States would not allow me to return to the States. I didn't dare cross the border through customs. As a young man I enjoyed a kind of dual citizenship. If you were born in the USA and never voted, taught school, and I guess maybe more things in Canada, you were still a USA citizen. We could go back and forth without a worry. In 1932 I came up to Northgate, North Dakota, crossed over and visited Louis a couple days and went back, no problem. I came over to Scobey, headed up to see my dad and the officer said, Are you a US citizen?" I said, "Yes." He said that I'd better fill out a form. When we got through he said, "I'll have to deport you or you won't get back." He done me a good turn. There were a few wives and husbands that got stuck on that and had to stay.

Dad gave Walter the land, which caused some hard feelings in the family. To me and Henry it made no difference. If I'd wanted it all I'd had to do was stay there and farm it; and he seemed to think a lot of me. Dad died alone in the hospital in Willow Bunch in July of 1947. As I told Hank, a man with five sons and a daughter should not have to die alone, but that was life at that time. I didn't think I could go into Canada, but they had changed the law again and I got to go to the funeral.

I done a lot of foolish things in my time. We had an old bobsled that I suppose was used to haul the furniture and things during the winter. I decided to gather it together, put a 125-bushel box on it and use it to haul wheat to Verwood, 35 miles away. I loaded a load of wheat and took off. Those old runners, they just caved in and the one bunk broke. They were too old for that kind of work. How I got there I can't imagine, but I did; and as luck would have it, they had an old bunk in an implement business there, and the runners were cast so the front part was iron. All I needed was a piece of hardwood 2x6, a new runner and bunk, and I had a good sleigh.

1928

In the winter of 1927-28, I took the train for Chicago. It was forty degrees below zero. The train was a mixed work and freight but we got to Assiniboia and the main line. Some people from northern Saskatchewan, where I had been in my wandering days, were on the train, so it wasn't too bad. I got to Minneapolis late in the evening and asked a cop where there was a good hotel. He said the one across the street was as good as any, so I got myself a bed and had some sleep.

While I was eating my breakfast the next morning, a man came in, sat down beside me, and started talking. I told him I was taking a train out that day. Strange to say, he was also going on that train. He wanted to get together for a while, as we would be taking the same train. He didn't look good to me, so I told him I had some letters to write and would be busy. Of course I had already told him that I had come off a ranch in Montana. He finally caught up to me again in the evening and insisted I go up to the Ritz Hotel with him. As it was only a block away I thought not much could happen. As we came in the door we were met by an Englishman, or supposed-to-be Englishman. He said, "Could you gentlemen tell me where the American Consul is?"

My so-called friend said, "No. We're strangers here, too; but come in and have a cup of coffee with us." Which he gladly did.

I was kind of puzzled for a while as to what was going to happen. Some way the conversation got around to matching, a game of chance using money. Of course the Englishman had matches. He either didn't know the game, or pretended he didn't. My friend explained what was meant by matching for money. The Englishman said that was a cinch, and he could do it every time. He had to go to the bathroom and my friend said, "Let's take him."

I said, "I guess not."

"Well, let's just teach him a lesson. He is so cocky."

The Englishman came back then, and the other man said, "Let's match."

I said, "I guess not." He insisted, but I said, "I'll pay for the coffee," and got up and left. I felt like I was being set up to be fleeced.

I took the train for Crandon, Wisconsin, as that was where my cousin, Annie, now lived. When I was let off the train in a little town about 2A.M., I didn't know what to do. Nothing was lighted, and I could see they were closing the depot. The man told me where I could get a room in a home there. I had breakfast there the next morning and went on to Crandon on a freight train. I stayed a few days, and then on to Chicago. I found my cousins there. They had three grocery stores, so I stayed with them a while and helped out. I helped sell and deliver Christmas trees. Once I had to deliver a large tree to a house and carry it up a spiral staircase. I wasn't sure I'd be able to get it up there, but somehow I did. I also did some cashiering in one of the stores.

Lydia was in Chicago then, which is mostly why I went there. She had written me once in the mid-twenties that she needed money, so I sent her $20. She never gave any address to send to, just general delivery. I got in touch with her and told her I wanted to go to see her. She said it was too far to come to where she lived, and for me to come to see her at work. She worked nights at 26th and Wentworth. My cousin told me not to go because that was a tough neighborhood. I said, "I won't take any money." She said, "They'll beat you up then."

I went. Lydia worked in a restaurant. A man there kept eyeing me, and it bothered me after what my cousin had said. I waited until he went to make a phone call. Then I said good-by and got out of there. There was a bunch of people waiting for a street car, but I took off for Halsted Street four blocks over, and was happy to get out of there.

Over the holidays, my cousins liked to get together and play poker. I decided I'd just excuse myself as I didn't have too much money to lose. Well, they played, and so did I. They played a three-cent limit. I was used to playing no limit, and lost two or three dollars. It wasn't my game.

I stayed in Chicago for a while, then went to Milwaukee, as we had some cousins there. I signed up in an electrical school. The school was to get me a job, which they finally did, in the tool shop of the Milwaukee Forge and Machine Shop. They made gears and different things for different companies. It was my job to sharpen and keep the tools in shape for those working in the shop. I went to night school and found it was pretty hard when I did not have the background education for what I had to learn. They did not question my educational background and my grades were all in the top nineties, but I could see there would come a time when I would not be able to do all the figuring. Hank wanted me to come back and help him, and as I had land there I had bought, I went back to Montana.

The Richland Pool Hall

In the spring of 1928, Hank wrote and wanted me to come back and help him with his farming. So, back to Montana. I had purchased three hundred twenty acres of land in 1926, not broke up. I helped Henry and broke up about fifty acres and seeded it to flax. I broke up another sixty-seven acres for the next year's crop.

In mid-summer I heard they were building a branch line out of Saco to go north of Harlem, so I thought I'd start some kind of business again. I don't know how I figured to raise enough money, but that didn't seem to bother me much. Walter and I took off one morning, as he had worked a summer or two in that part of the country. We got to Saco and I started following the survey line, as they hadn't started any building yet. We stayed at a ranch the first night, and went on the next day. As no town had been laid out at Turner or Hogland, there wasn't much we could do. We got back to Chinook and stayed overnight in Malta. We started off the next morning and stopped at the hot water wells at Saco. At that time there was just a trench where the water ran away from the well, with a tank farther down where you could take a bath, which we did. I got a good headache as we were down wind and there was gas in the water.

We got lost coming back as it got dark, and we landed in Richland, a busy little town with people everywhere. It looked like a good place to start a pool hall. There had been a place there, but the owner had women and liquor, so they shut him up and put him away for a year or two. I went to Plentywood to see if I could buy the building, but the owner would not sell it for a pool hall. It had been raining and the roads were not too good. I took the wrong road out of Redstone, which was easy to do, got lost and finally decided to just go to sleep until daylight. A man came along and I told him where I wanted to go. He said, "You're going the wrong way," and gave me some way to go. But I waited for daylight, got turned around, and finally got to Whitetail; and 8A.M. I got home.

I decided to build, which I did. This is hard to believe, because I had no money. I did have money coming to me from different people, just notes. I made a deal for the lumber, bought a lot and hired three men to put up the building. The carpenter was to get one dollar an hour and the other two got fifty cents an hour. I went to the bank and asked for $200. The bank president said no. I talked to the cashier. He also said no. One day I stopped by the bank. These two men were not around but Bob Holland was. He was in charge of loans. I had purchased some horses from him at different times, and he knew I would pay back what I owed. He asked me what I needed. I said I needed $200. He gave it to me. I bet that cashier was put out. They got even with me. When my note was due, they never said a word, just waited until there was enough money in my checking account and took it out to cover the loan.

Henry Sr. in front of Mel's Building

Richland was a pretty wild town. There seemed to be something going on all the time. When I first opened up the pool hall, we were sitting, playing poker. About three in the morning, we saw a car drive by slowly. We thought nothing of it. Then three masked men came in and held us up. I did not lose much as I had very little on hand. But two men who had been harvesting and had their fall earnings with them, as they were planning to go back to Oklahoma the next day, lost everything. Of course, I lost also, as I cashed a check for them so they could get home. I was never repaid. After this incident the townsmen got together and hired a man as night watchman in town. We paid him $150 for a month, then we gave up. We couldn't afford to pay him. I bought his pistol which I still have somewhere.

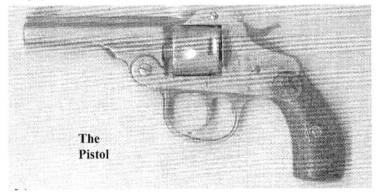

The Pistol

One night three local boys went to Peerless to a dance. They picked up the three wild Whipple sisters, one only fifteen years old, and brought them back to Richland. They kept them in a shack, intending to take them on to Glentana to a dance the next night. They had to get food for the girls from the restaurant so they were found out. They were arrested on most any kind of charge that could be drummed up, including white slavery. Mr. Beachler had been a JP or something, and had some law books, so he was the judge. Howard Gaffney was defending the boys; and a stranger, a blockman for a farm machine manufacturing company, prosecuted. We had quite a trial. It ended with the boys having to pay John Mortenson fifteen dollars to take the girls home. The next morning Howard G. dressed up in an old coat and shot a couple of shots. The guys told the boys that the girls' dad was in town looking for them. This went on 'till noon. By the time they were finished with them, the boys were hiding out in the top room of the elevator, pretty scared. One of the girls later came back and stayed with a bachelor.

Mike Gustitus ran a poker game for me, not legal, of course; but we had an honest and quiet game so we got by. One night, Sailor Johnson was pretty drunk and was trying to pick a fight with Mike, going around the snooker table to get a ball to throw at Mike. So they took him out and tied him up; and it was winter, too.

Mike and I played cards one night. About daybreak, we decided to go to Wood Mountain as there was a rodeo dance and what-have-you. When we arrived at Wood Mountain, they had not got their beer yet. Mike wanted some beer, so we went to New Wood Mountain to get some. The States were still dry at that time, I believe. We got back to Wood Mountain, and as it was quite warm, took off out coats; also my small amount of money, and locked them in Mike's car. We wandered around the grounds until the dance started. Mike saw a woman who took his eye. Having spent part of my life in Canada, I knew the man she was dancing with. Mike was married and his wife was home. I tried to discourage him, but he made it on his own. He disappeared and I never saw him again until noon the next day. It seemed this lady was with five more women, wives without their husbands. They had a big tent, and so Mike said they just drank beer and talked. But, meanwhile, I sure put in a bad night. It got cold and the wind came up and me with no coat or money. The doings was some distance from town, so I just walked around trying to keep warm. Along toward morning, I found a car I had sold to my dad's neighbor. I crawled in to get out of the wind and maybe lay down on the seat to rest, as I had not slept for two nights. Some time later, another person came along and got in. I thought he maybe wanted to sleep and maybe had more right to the car than I had, so I got out and walked around again trying to keep warm.

Another time, I took a friend and we went to Wood Mountain. We got tired of what was going on, so headed back home. On the way to Opheim, we caught up with three girls walking back toward the States. They were from Wolf Point. We picked them up. My car was a coupe. My friend was a very quiet and very bashful man. He sure didn't like having three girls piled on and around him. When we got to the customs we were in trouble. The officers didn't like it that we picked the girls up, and were about to make us take them back. They let them go through customs, however, and we dropped them off in Opheim.

Before my time, Snooze Larsen, one of our mostly drunk citizens, lined nine men against a wall at gunpoint. No one was hurt.

We had a doing of some kind going on which lasted the night through. Somewhere along, two local farmers got involved some way. One took the other man's hat and put it down the outhouse toilet hole. We had two groups of men busy keeping them apart until they got sober.

1929-1930

Business in the pool hall was good. Come spring, I sold my Chevrolet coupe and bought a new car. 1929 wasn't too bad. Things started to tighten up later in 1930.

My dad was always looking for gold. He wanted to go to the Little Rockies to prospect. We got to Zortman just about sunset and drove up a mountain. Then it got dark and I didn't know where I was. We drove around for a while. There being forty or more miles to any town, we slept in the car. Come morning, we got in the mountains again and started up a canyon. I followed a trail up the side of the mountain, straddling ruts a foot deep. I don't know how we would have gotten out of there if I had fallen into one. Dad finally gave up and we went home tired and hungry.

In the early part of the summer, I got a couple of letters from Lydia one day. She said she was in trouble and I should come and help her out. Nothing different. Got in the car and headed for Canada. I was a little late getting to customs, but I knew them real well and they were still open.

The Canadian customs officer said, "I'm sorry, but I'll have to search your car," which he did. I had nothing in it. He said he hadn't expected to find anything, but someone had reported that I was hauling contraband. I used to go across the border a lot, so the person who reported me may have figured that I might be smuggling. If I had been, my car would have been confiscated and they would have gotten ten percent of whatever it would have brought in sale.

I got home, and as none of us had too much ready cash, Dad went to the bank and borrowed $500. I took $100 of my own; and Walter, Mary, Bill, Fanny and I took off for Chicago in Walter's new Whippet car. It rained all the way to Chicago. It started to rain as we left Scobey; and we got down to Louie's place at North Gate late at night, a rough day's drive in mud for what is now only three or four hours. After we got to Kenmare we got in more gravel and it went better. Most of the roads in those days were gravel. Very few roads had pavement, and even those were very narrow.

Somewhere in Wisconsin, some men were standing around a kind of barricade in the road. It was dark. I was driving. Walter said, "Don't stop. It might be a holdup." We went around the barricade. It turned out that the road was under construction, being rebuilt. We were lucky enough to find a road to town.

Walter was driving as we were going into a small town. A man was walking on the shoulder of the road. He got too far out into the road, and it appeared that Walter hit him. We looked back and he was up and coming, so Walter never stopped.

With just a few problems, we got to Milwaukee, stopped and saw our cousins there, then took off for Chicago. On Sundays or holidays the traffic was thick, as there were no freeways then, just two lanes. We got to Des Plaines in the evening with one dim light. The other light had burned out. We were stopped and told we could go no further until we got it fixed.

In Chicago, we went to an old hotel and got a couple of rooms. It was in a bad part of town and we discovered it was some kind of gang hangout so we wanted to leave. The hotel wouldn't refund our money, so I took our money and slept in the car to guard the car and the money. The rest all went into one room and got by the best they could.

Mary had a sister living in southeast Chicago. We had to go through Chicago to get there. It took us hours to get through downtown Chicago, but in time we got there. The next day we started looking for Lydia. Now, I wonder why one would even think of trying to find someone in Chicago with no address and no leads, but we did. We tried the police station and about every place we could think of, and after a week, we found her. Now I'd like to know how we did it, but I don't remember.

She had a room in a house and had two daughters, three and five years old. As she couldn't take care of them and support them, the authorities were going to take them from her. This was the problem she had written about. If she had told me this, or given me an address, it would have been a lot easier. Well, we gathered up what she had, promised to pay her back rent (It never got paid.), and started home.

We went to Louis' place and left her there. They got her a job keeping house for some bachelor, which was fine for a while. Because she was in Canada and wanted to get back to Chicago, she got it into her head that she should go back to the USA. She had a little money by now, I suppose, and she got a room in North Gate and was staying there.

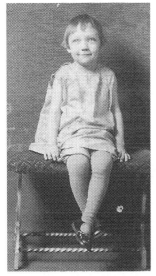

Esther

Louie called me and I went down the next morning. There wasn't much we could do, as it seemed she had moved out and was determined not to go back. We got together with the sheriff and county attorney, but, as she had not been a resident long enough, they said they couldn't do anything. Also, it was election time.

We decided to bring her back to Henry's place in Montana and work from there. She agreed to that, and she stayed there a couple of months without any problem. Then she started hearing voices again. One winter day she took the girls out without coats and walked for several miles.

We talked to the sheriff and attorney, and they decided she should

Audrey

be sent to Warm Springs, Montana's mental institution. Then I got a shock. Because Lydia trusted me, they thought I should be the one to talk her into going into town. So we went out, and some way I convinced her that she should come to town with the girls. Of course, the hearing had all been decided beforehand, and they took her to Warm Springs. I felt like I had betrayed her. She was in Warm Springs from 1930-1942.

Now we had two little girls to look after. We made a deal with the Henry Halversons to keep them for thirty-five dollars a month. As there were five of us boys, we were to each pay seven dollars a

month. Well, I paid twenty-eight of it, and I guess Hank paid his seven. I paid for about eighteen months. The girls were with Henry Halverson for about one and a half years during 1929-30. After that they stayed with several other families: another Halverson, the Nessees, Oliver Olsen, and the Jack Baldrys. Then they stayed with me from 1936-1939 until I moved to Portland. After that Audrey boarded with Mrs. Vance in return for a grocery bill they hadn't paid. Esther went to Opheim to high school and boarded there. Audrey

Melvin with Esther and Audrey, 1936

went to Portland in '41-'42 and went to high school there. She stayed in Scobey with Hank and Lydia after that until she married. She graduated from high school in Scobey.

Along towards the spring of 1930 business got pretty slow. I had made a debt of $600 to General Motors when I purchased my car in 1929. I was paying fifty dollars a month. I was unable to make some of the payments. Joe Sours was the section foreman on the railroad. Joe had come from Germany to Winnipeg, Manitoba. He walked across the border to the USA but never went through immigration. Many years later when he was in Richland they caught up with him. It had been so long they let him go. He could not read or write, nor could he keep his crew's time or bookwork. He got one of the men in town to do that for him. When he was to go in for his exams, he always managed to be sick. He finally lost out when a man got killed. I guess there were questions. I wasn't in Richland at the time. I asked Joe if he would pick up my three car payments until my business picked up. He did. Joe seemed to think that when the last payment was made the car was his. He had never said anything to make me aware that he thought this way. If he had I would have made other arrangements. I had to come up with a hundred, fifty dollars now or a car, so Joe seemed to think. I went up to Canada to see if Walter or Bill had any loose change. Walter had none, but Bill owed me for a horse he had gotten from me. I had gotten the horse from a man who owed me money but couldn't pay. This was a common problem in those days. Bill had pigs and Walter knew where he could borrow a Ford truck. We loaded up a load of pigs. About 3 a.m. we started out for Moose Jaw. It was a very dark morning. It seemed that with this model truck, if you missed a gear when shifting, you lost everything: motor, brakes, lights, etc. Some people dragged a 4x4 behind so if they missed a shift they would not go rolling back downhill. We came to a hill at Scout Lake. They were graveling the road and they had gravel dumped along the side of the road. Walter went to shift up and missed gears. Away we went

coasting down the hill. No lights, no brakes. I stood on the running board to help guide him so he wouldn't run into the gravel piles. It was so dark I couldn't see very well. How he got that truck to the bottom of that mile-long hill, I don't know. But he did. The wind came up and it was hard to see the road. Some time that day we sold the pigs and got back. I think I still had to borrow a hundred dollars from O. B. Egland. I paid Joe and he bought a new car.

Audrey and husband Ron, Esther
Lydia
1985

60

1931-1932

I sold the pool hall to Frank Laffenase in 1931. No money down, of course, and I never got any either. He was to pay for the stock and pay rent on the building. He never paid anything toward rent, nor did he pay anything on the stock. He eventually walked away from the pool hall and went to Opheim. No one had any money in those days. Mike Gustitus came back to Richland sometime later and opened the pool hall back up while he was waiting for the Fort Peck Dam to open. Frank was upset about that, because, he said he had intended to open it again. He was a little late.

My friend, Heine, and I took off for Bieber, California, as a railroad was going there from Klamath Falls. Heine was a shipwright and carpenter, and was wanting to find some work. I was also interested in finding some work. I had my Chev coupe and a tent, and everything else we needed was put into the back of the car. We got to Fort Benton the first day. We pitched our tent in a park. The next morning I went down to the creek, broke the ice, and got our water. The coffee was the best we had on our whole trip. We went on to Great Falls and then to Butte. The next day we got a cabin in Butte and stayed over a day, looking around.

We went to see Lydia in Warm Springs. She told me she'd had a hearing and they had asked her if she still heard the voices. She said, "Yes," so they would not let her go. She told me, "They'll never get me on that one again." I decided I couldn't help her as she wasn't going to be honest, and I never did. Hank finally went good for her and got her out, but many years later.

The next day we went on to Dillon and over to Bannock. As Roosevelt had raised the price of gold, the gold mines were being opened again. Butte had sent along a bunch of women, and gambling was in full swing. We saw a cabin a mile or so out of town where the sage was cleared away a little. It didn't look like anyone was living there, so we drove a spike in a log and proceeded to set up our tent. A man rode up on a horse and moved us out of there in a hurry. We went into town, looked around, and talked with some of the men. It didn't seem like a good place to look for work, so we decided to move on. We went across country toward the highway to Salt Lake City. That night we pitched our tent in front of a house where the sidewalk should have been. The people were very nice to us. We got water from their tap. Of course we did not build a fire.

The next day we went on to Salt Lake City, and here again we got a cabin and stayed over a day. Then on to Las Vegas, stopping somewhere over night. I don't remember where. We got to Las Vegas and got a cabin or maybe pitched our tent. We looked the town over. There was gambling everywhere. As soon as you walked up to a table someone would offer to go in with you for fifty cents, a gimmick to try to draw people into the game. They were playing Pan which is more of a disease than a game. We didn't have any money to throw away gambling.

The next morning we drove out toward the dam site. Nothing was happening there yet. No work. We went back in the afternoon. Then we left for Fresno where Heine's sister lived. That night we made our bed out on the sand. I never thought of snakes or fleas, but anyway, they were there. They didn't bother us. We went on to Fresno and stayed a few days there with Heine's sister. Her husband's family had an orchard there.

We left for Bieber. We had a broken spring, which we had to stop and fix. It was not too serious, just a couple dollars for a new leaf. In Bieber, as was usual in those days, more people were wandering around looking for work than there was work to be had. So we got the usual cold reception.

We left Bieber and headed toward Oregon. On the way, we stopped in a little town where there was a Y in the road, and a couple of big fig trees. We thought it would not be a bad place to sleep. Along toward morning Heine woke up and started digging around in the blankets. He said, "I think I've lost my pants!"

I got to digging and I said, "You've got nothing on me. I've lost mine." As it happened, it was a warm evening and we had moved up in our blankets, and of course, our pants were still farther down.

We crossed the Columbia River at Umatilla on the Patterson Ferry. It cost us one dollar. Then on toward home. The road through the Rockies by Glacier Park was barely passable, but we made it through somehow. Home. We were gone a month and it cost us $95. We had $5 left out of the $100 we started with.

Heine applied for a job delivering mail. He got it. It didn't pay much, but it was a living.

Right after Heine and I got back from California, Clarence White talked Madds Ibsen and me into going down to the Jordan country to look for gold, as he had heard an old legend about some gold there. So, again we got a tent and whatnot and took off. We camped on the prairie the first night. The next day, driving along, we saw a bunch of sage hens. Madds had to shoot one. We got to the Missouri River and pitched our tent, and I cooked that sage hen, but we couldn't eat it. Too much sage. We tossed the hen into the river.

A rancher there had some set line and a live box (a holding box for live fish). We got our hen back in catfish. We had fish all the time, and things were not too bad until it started raining. Sitting in a tent listening to the rain never appealed to me. We camped there for about two weeks. We had to wait for things to dry out because the road out followed a narrow ridge from which we did not want to slip. We never found the gold we were looking for, but the day before we left we caught a sturgeon about four feet long. We wrapped it in some canvas and laid it on the running board, wetting it down good. I guess Clarence's family enjoyed it.

Working in Minnesota

Then Madds talked to one of his sisters, who had just come back from Minneapolis. She said we might get a job in Minnesota working on a road crew building retaining walls, as two of the men were going to leave. Howard White, Ed Lawrence, Madds, and myself took off. Howard White and Ed Lawrence were going to North Dakota to pick potatoes. We went in Madd's car. We stopped in a little town in North Dakota and got up early for a good start. Ed and Madds went into town to get gas or something. Howard and I waited. About eight o'clock they came back. They had found something besides what they went to get. Madds was going to drive but, happy to say, Ed said, "If you're going to drink, you get in the back seat with me and let the boys drive." We dropped Howard and Ed off in a little town northwest of Fargo. Madds and I slept in the car, which we had fixed so that we could let the front seat down to make a bed. Howard stayed in North Dakota for several years, working on farms there.

Madds and I got to Granite Falls, Minnesota, where the work was. The boss, Chris, was a Dane and so was Madds. This was to be to our advantage in getting a job. It seems that Madds wasn't going to have any problem getting work, but Chris didn't seem too concerned about giving me a job. A couple of days later one of the boys who was leaving told me why I hadn't been hired. He said Madds had told Chris that I had never worked – just ran a pool hall. So I was stranded. I had borrowed $15 from Art Hanson before I left, as I was out of money; and, as I said before, there were no payments coming in from the pool hall or anywhere else

Northern States Power had just finished building their plant, and everyone seemed to be looking for work. I picked up a little change once in a while, and then Chris needed someone to unload a railroad carload of sand. They had a kind of trip box you filled. When the truck came you just tipped it into the truck and filled it again. It was 110 degrees in the shade. The crew on the job had just quit because of the heat. But the truck driver kept coming, and I kept on shoveling and making frequent trips to the well, which had very cold water. I got so sick I couldn't eat anything for about three days. This, of course, didn't help me much in getting a job.

There was a bunch of Russians there working in the rock. I was told they might need someone. Although they didn't need help, they asked me if I had ever driven a mule. I walked down to the river to watch the mule work. It was an old International tractor without lugs.

It slid off the bank and was helpless. I really didn't want to drive that mule.

Later in the fall, Chris' crew wanted to work on Sunday. The regular truck driver supposedly had hurt his hand. I never quite believed he did. He was trying to get the insurance company to pay him for it. The young guy who was filling in for the driver, had one too many on Saturday night, so he was in no condition to work on Sunday. Chris let me drive truck that day, and from that time on I got along good with him.

Madds wasn't really wanting work. It turns out he was the one who had never worked. His father ran the John Deere store in Scobey, and he had helped him out some in the store. The construction work was harder than what he wanted to do. He left and went to work for someone a few miles from where we were, to oversee, he said.

Sometime in February, 1932, I came back to Montana on the train to get my car. I went over to Henry's and he took me down to the creek. From there I walked over to John Schaeffer's place in Canada, a distance of about six or eight miles. I stayed there overnight. The next night they were going up to Jim Shatron's place, the old Dave White ranch; so I went along and finished the night there. The next day I walked up to Kessler's, which was about nine miles. I stayed there overnight and went on to Dad's. The next day I planned to go over to Bill's; but they came along and were going to Wagner's, Fannie's folks. So I said good-bye to Dad and went with them. I don't remember how long I stayed there, but I went back to John Schaeffer's again another night, and then walked back to the USA. I got to the creek and was afraid to cross, as the water was moving under the ice. I was afraid I'd break through. The Jack Baldrys were living in the Dave Tingley house at that time, close by. So Baldry came and threw a rope across to me and I got across the ice all right. I went back to Henry's and on to Richland again. I stayed a few days.

There was an all-night party at Ray Varsnick's place, with cards, and Tom and Jerrys. I didn't get any sleep, but took off the next morning anyway. One of the Hersel boys from North Dakota was with me. It was a nice, sunshiny morning, but not for long. It was thawing and sloppy for a ways, then it started to storm. The chains I had for the car were worn out. I got stuck once and had to be pulled out. But we finally got to Nashua about four o'clock that afternoon. Now we were on Highway #2 and thought we had it made.

The car got a flat tire and it sure was cold changing it, but we got to Williston, North Dakota that first day. My partner wanted to go on.

We started to go and ran into a big snowdrift, so I said, "No more for me." We went back and got a room. The next morning we had to wait for the plows to open the roads. The plow went halfway to Minot and met the plow coming from the other direction. Then we were able to go again.

We got to the Hersel farm. Hersel wanted me to go on in and stay, but I did not want to, and I went on. As I came into a little town, I saw a man who had driven into the cemetery to turn around, and had gotten stuck. He asked me to send someone to pull him out. I stopped in a restaurant to have something to eat, and told the waitress there was a man up in the cemetery who wanted someone to pull him out. I guess she thought I was joking. It took some talking to convince them.

I stayed in Jamestown over night. Hersel had given me three dollars for letting him ride with me. Except for the three dollars, I was broke by the time I got to Jamestown. I guess I would have had a rough time if he hadn't given me those three dollars. I lived on credit until spring.

I didn't get work until about May. I went to work for Chris again. We, Chris' crew, stayed in Granite Falls for about six weeks. We were rip-rapping a road bank along the river. That is, we laid rock along the river bank. We were paid one dollar a week, I think, for a room in a private home; and meals cost us thirty-five cents in the restaurant in Granite Falls.

From Granite Falls we went to Erskine, Minnesota, where we had a job putting in drains on the highway, and extending culverts. I had a busy summer driving the truck hauling cement, water and gravel. I worked sometimes ninety or ninety-five hours a week, but I never put down more than eighty hours on my time. The work was there and I did it. I kept my own time. I don't know if I was really doing Chris a favor. Probably not, as the truck I was driving belonged to Chris. It was a partnership and he was getting paid for the use of the truck based on the amount of time it was used.

Over Labor Day, a friend and I took off for Minneapolis. We stopped and had a cup of coffee; took a look at the gas gage on the tank. It was about two-thirds full, so we thought we had plenty. But the car was leaning when we checked the gage, and pretty soon we started looking for a town with gas. We thought we had one, according to the map. But it wasn't there. Finally we stopped at a farm and the farmer gave us some gas. Or maybe it was kerosene. Because money was short, he carried a gallon of kerosene in his car in case he ran out of gas. While his car was warm it would keep running.

Once, Bill, the mixer man, was to go with me to Minneapolis to help me. We had the mixer on the old truck and were pulling the boss's camper. We came to a town. A sign read, "Road Closed, Construction." Bill said, "Oh, that's all right. We can go through there." We got out a ways, and they had filled the road with sand and some tar mixed with it. We got into this mess about fifty feet and there we were. With the camper behind, we couldn't back up. We finally went up to a farm and the farmer came down with four horses and pulled us back out. We spent the night there. He showed us a detour so we made it to Minneapolis.

We finished our job in the fall. All the boys except myself and one other guy took off to celebrate. The two of us hauled in the material and cleaned up the job. It took us about three days; and when we got through, the boys were done drinking and wanted to help. They were unhappy that we had done it all, but I didn't feel too sorry for them.

Melvin on bridge above Granite Falls on the Minnesota River, 1932

Then we got a job at Red Wing, putting in the footing for a steel bridge into a man's yard. There was a bunkhouse at Hay Creek which four or five of us slept in. It was a double bunk deal. I slept on a top bunk, and always put my clothes behind me. The rest of the men left their clothes on the floor. One night somebody crept in there and took all their money. It was a sad morning, as winter was coming on and their savings were gone.

We moved into Red Wing then, and got room and board for $4.50 a week. We were getting four dollars a day, forty cents an hour for working ten hours a day. Of course, most of the time I got in more time.

It was pretty cold just before Christmas, about fourteen below, no wind. We went to work. The boss said, "No more!" He got a thermometer so he would know how cold it was and not go out again in the cold. Of course, I had felt the damp cold before it got so cold and had on a lot of clothes. The guys asked me what I was going to do when it got cold. I told them that when it got cold enough to freeze the moisture out of the air I'd be fine.

1933

Over New Year's, 1933, Chris and most of our crew (There were nine of us.) went to Minneapolis. Just three of us stayed behind. We had a make-shift building over our job and we had to keep fires going. New Year's night a high wind came up and blew down our building, which was made out of 2x2's and sisal craft paper. So we had to get busy and get it rebuilt before the inspector came around. It was a nice day and we managed to get what we needed and got it up in time. If it had stayed cold and froze, the inspector would have condemned the job and we would have had to take it down and start over. When we finished that job we moved back to Minneapolis.

In the winter of 1933 I saw an ad in the paper for a farm job. The man at the employment agency told me it was a cow-milking set-up. I told him it was no use for me to go down there, as I could not milk. I had bad wrists. He talked me into going and I paid him two dollars. The farmer and I went cutting wood and he told me of his troubles with his other man. I told him that I was no improvement, as I couldn't milk many cows. He said, "No problem." He'd milk some, his wife would milk some, his twelve-year-old girl would milk some, and I could milk some. I stayed there two or three months, until spring; and I thought Chris might get a job and we could go to work. There was no work.

The year of 1933 was a bad one. I got a small job, which took a week or so. Then I went to the World's Fair in Chicago with my boss, Chris, and his family. I had relatives there so it didn't cost me too much.

Back in Minnesota, while driving around by the Mississippi River one day, I noticed that the riverbed was full of gravel. We got permission to go through a private yard for ten cents a load, and put an ad in the paper: "Driveway Gravel for Sale." I guess we got a couple dollars a load, and shoveled it by hand. I also hauled landscape sod in Minneapolis. Then I talked Chris into letting me take the truck down to Austin on a dirt-hauling job. No good, as we got paid by the mile. We got a short haul and their own truck got the long one.

Richland Again

As winter was approaching, I pulled out for Montana. Things were pretty bad in Montana at that time, but construction on the Fort Peck Dam was supposed to begin, so I thought I might be all right. But, like all good prospects for work, it was slow getting going. Mike Gustitus and I went down to Fort Peck to see how things were going, but all they were doing at that time was clearing out brush. I took some bedding with me, and as I thought I'd be going back, I left it in the shack where we stayed. Nothing was going on so we went back to Richland. As I did not go back to Fort Peck, and did not even know who we stayed with, I lost my bedding.

After Frank left the pool hall, Mike had come back and opened it. He was running it when I got back from Minnesota in 1933. Joe Sours was sleeping in my bed. Joe was supposed to have epilepsy. I had had one experience with that, and it was enough. I took a couple of blankets and moved down to one of the pool tables. Joe followed me down, so I didn't get away from him. All I had gained was that I was sleeping on a hard pool table instead of my bed. One morning Joe got up about four in the morning and lit all the gas lights. I asked him what he was going to do. "Scrub the floor," he said. I told him that it was only four A.M., we used the depot's mop, and they would not open until eight. He laid back down on the pool table and went to sleep. After I started the grocery store, I told him he'd have to find somewhere else to sleep because the stock belonged to Ben and he did not want anyone sleeping in there. Joe did not like it but he had to go. I lied a little, but it was the only way I knew of to get him out. I don't think I ever refused anyone a place to sleep, except for this instance. Sometimes we were four to a bed but we managed. Someone told me once that I never turned anyone down for credit. I think he might be right. Poor people will pay if they can, and usually find a way. In my books, it's the big income person you had to wait on or forget.

Shortly after this Joe started a Beechler store in competition with me. He purchased his stock from Getchel's in Scobey and did fairly well with the store, because I didn't have the money to buy seasonal produce. Because of his lack of education, he wasn't a good businessman, and once I was able to build up my stock, he had to quit the grocery business. He later, after we had left Richland, went into a restaurant with Myrtle's sister. It was not very well run either.

1934

In the spring of 1934 I made a deal with a man in Scobey, Ben Schaik, and started a grocery store in my building in Richland. This was something new but, in time, I learned something about food. When I started the store, my deal with Ben was that he would furnish the stock and I would put in my time. I had no money as I had very little work in 1933. I had to borrow twenty dollars to pay the freight because the stock was shipped by rail from Scobey to Richland. There were three things about the deal I did not like: (1) Ben wanted to send the groceries. Sometimes I was selling more of an item than he had in stock and could not get enough of the item to satisfy my customers. Sometimes he would buy something he could not sell in Scobey, like fire crackers, and I would end up with those items. (2) Purchasing from him, I was not able to take advantage of volume discounts that were offered in those days. (3) Ben was a Jew and some people did not want their money to go to a Jew. Why, I don't know. We had no papers and I always said my word was as good as my signature, but I could see no future for either of us.

Ben came out to help me get started, as this was something different for me again. We slept upstairs over the store. During the night, we heard some silver money hit the floor. Ben jumped out of bed, grabbed a shoe, and started to pound the floor. I got up and opened the window which was over the store's door. The thief was just going out as I got the window opened, and he escaped. Over the years someone had gotten a key to the place.

Ben sent a young man out for two weeks to help me to learn the grocery business. The store had not been opened for business yet. One night there was something going on in Opheim. We decided to go. It was in the spring of the year and there were no good roads. We got a couple miles out of town and got stuck by the creek. We went back to the store and to bed. After a while he said he was not feeling well, or at least he said something to let me know things were not right I didn't know what his problem was. Then he wanted to go downstairs and outside. It was a nice spring evening. We stood out there for a while, then he said, "Let's go in." We went inside and upstairs and stood there for a few minutes. He said, "I must have had a spell." He told me that if it happened again, to grab the first thing I could get my hands on and stuff it in his mouth, even a dirty sock, to keep him from biting his tongue.

Later in the summer, after the store had been opened for business, a man brought a small beef in. I think he had run the animal some. My icebox wasn't set up to hang meat in. The meat was poor quality. All in all, the experiment wasn't too good money-wise. But it got me interested in handling meat. My first ice box was a cupboard that Hans Scott, Hilda Stahl's father, gave me. It had large doors on it that could be opened up to put a beef in to hang. Later I built an icebox out of a coal shed that was attached to the back of the store. I put a ceiling in the shed, tinned it so it would hold water, and made a hole in the top for ice to be dropped in. The problem with it was that it would freeze the meat in the winter if I didn't crack the door open a bit. I got a butcher's block and tried to figure one cut from another. I butchered a lot of beef in the next few years.

One time Ben was using his car to deliver some stock to me. His car broke down and he charged the repairs to my store. I did not feel that was right, but ended up paying for it.

In the fall of 1934, George Killenbeck, who had the garage in Richland, wanted to hone out my car engine and put new pistons in it. For this he wanted fifteen dollars. I wasn't interested as the car had taken me over most of the country and had done its job. He talked me into it as there was no work for the shop in winter. They just wanted something to do. They got the job done and come spring I went to Fort Peck with a load of eggs. The motor was making an awful noise, so when I got back to Glasgow I had it looked at. They told me I needed new valve guides. My valve guides were loose because of more compression from the new pistons. I got that taken care of. One Sunday I was out driving and the crank shaft broke. Well George was busy with spring business by now and said it wasn't worth fixing. I told him he had talked me into my problem in the first place, and to go and put in the shaft. Two months or so later Ole, his helper, drove the car over and parked it in front of the store. George and his wife were on vacation. Come Sunday I drove to Scobey and once again there was a terrible racket. I got someone to take the car to Scobey to Hagfelt's garage. There were seven bearings which hadn't been tightened. Well, I was getting pretty angry by now; so when George's wife came in to the store, I asked where Ole was. She said he was on vacation. I said, "That's a good place to keep him." George came over and said, "If you have something to say, you say it to me and not my wife." I told him I didn't care. Whoever came in first was to hear it. I lost a customer.

I sent groceries out with the mailman in the winter, as some people had a hard time getting to town. The roads were not good and you had to have horses, and plan to maybe have to stay in town overnight. And of course, the mail must go through, that is, if possible. One morning a rancher came in and said he wanted to charge a few things. He had been playing poker all night and was somewhat drunk. I told him I had to get the box of groceries to the post office first. The mail left at eight o'clock. I guess, being in the condition he was in, he misunderstood me. He threw a couple articles on the counter with some change and walked out. He never came back. We would meet and talk. He said, "You apologize, I'll trade with you." I said that I had nothing to apologize for and explained the situation to him. That wasn't good enough. He drove to another town for his food. He had sheep, and when he had a crew for shearing, the man running his business for him bought the groceries from us. At that time the government had a loan bank set up. They gave the farmer or rancher just what he needed for his bills and no more. The farmer would present his bill to the loan bank and they gave him the money to pay it. This created a rob Peter to pay Paul situation. The farmer would get behind and use the money meant for one bill to pay an older one which should have been paid before. We knew what was going on but knew we'd get paid in time, although that was not the case with this man. I think the man who handled his money took care to see it got where it should go. This system saved a lot of ranchers as they couldn't waste any money unless there was some left over somewhere.

Another time a bachelor farmer named Bill came in and picked up some things. He was quite a kidder. He had some credit coming from a check he left with us. I don't know why I said it, but I said, "Oh, that's enough for the old bill." He said to his nephew, "Let's go get the mail." He never came back again. After he left the store he got to thinking of what I said. He was quite a gunman, and a year or two later on the men in town told me Bill had said, "I think I should bump Melvin off some night."

I had a customer who was still on a cash basis. He paid for his groceries with cash. One time, when he was harvesting the little crop they had in those days, he ordered some meat. As I was going by his place collecting or looking at beef or whatever I was doing, I dropped the meat off and charged it to him. When I asked him for the money he got mad and said he always paid cash. I couldn't get him to understand what had happened. Another customer lost. But in all cases it was their loss as much as mine, because they had to drive farther out to another town to buy their groceries, and sometimes you just need a small item.

I was in business four years during a depression time when people had no money, just forty-four dollars a month when there was a project or job available to work on. I had open charge accounts, and when I left Richland I had less than one hundred dollars due me. People were honest and most paid if they could do it.

Chris, the man I had worked for in Minnesota, wrote and wanted me to come back and work for him, but I had already started the store in Richland. He was going to put me on as straw boss. I don't think I could have worked for him anyway. Roosevelt had a law passed that all help had to be local.

1935

In the fall of 1935, I broke off my deal with Ben and went on my own. This is the only time in my life I did not see a deal through. I had been paying him for the stock as I sold it, but still owed on the stock in the store. I told him to take the stock and leave me the fixtures. He brought two trucks and hauled the goods back to Scobey. I paid him what I owed him and, of course, had no money left. The wholesale house would give me credit on a weekly basis, no long term. Now I wonder how one could even think of it, and how I managed I don't know. After a couple months, I was on C.O.D. with one wholesale house, Nash Finch; and, of course, we were charging to our customers. It sure wasn't easy. But, some way, I made it, and with time could pay my way.

I had a girl helping me in the store. We boarded in the restaurant for twenty-five dollars a month for the two of us. We both ate whatever was on the menu.

There was no welfare or government help of any kind in those days. In 1935 the WPA (Works Projects Administration) was created to put unemployed people to work on public projects during the depression of the 1930's. They built toilets and graveled roads, all by hand; and shoveled the gravel on and off the truck. If people could come up with a project, the money seemed to be there for it. The pay was forty-four dollars a month. They were going to build a dam at Richland. An irrigation ditch was dug for some miles and things were going good. Business at my store improved during this time. Then they decided there was too much gravel, or some other problem, and the project ended.

Melvin Rolandson had a bar next door to my store. There was always a lot of noise coming from there, sometimes for days at a time. We never paid any attention to the noise. There was also a building across the street that was a bar downstairs and had rooms for rent upstairs (hotel) with an outside back stair entry. One morning one of the drinking farmers, an Edland who lived about seven miles south of Richland, was found dead down below the hotel landing. It was supposed to look like he had fallen down from the landing and killed himself. He had a hole in his head, but there was nothing on the ground around there that could have caused the hole. It was assumed that there had been foul play; that the man had been killed in a fight at the bar next door, and the body moved to make it look like he had accidentally killed himself. The sheriff was from Glasgow and not familiar with the community around Richland. He asked us if we had heard anything from next door. We told him we had not heard anything more than was normal. He was mad. We thought he suspected one of the Fossum brothers who were big men. He said, "That bull of a moose has everybody scared." We really couldn't help him any. Andrew Fossum got sick a few weeks later, and died. The crime was never solved, as those who were in the bar would say nothing.

1936

I had a fire in the store in 1936. Glenda Fossum was working for me. I had some rooms up over the store, and had a kerosene stove there as Dad stayed with me quite a bit. We did some cooking up there when he was with me. Glenda lit the stove to heat some water to wash the counter. These stoves would flare up a high flame if not watched, which it did then. It was next to the wall and something hanging there caught fire. Glenda came running down the stairs screaming, "Fire!" and ran right out onto the street. I did not get too excited because I thought I could go up and throw a blanket over it and smother it out. It was so hot I couldn't get farther than the top of the stairs. It was a cool, misty morning so I guess there were more people in town than there normally was. One group formed a bucket line to the well near by. They went up the back stairs and threw the water as far as they could. Another group cut a hole in the roof and poured water down on the fire. We got it out with very little damage except for the upstairs: my bed, and some other things up there.

Roy Hanson, the International Implement dealer, had his building next to mine and they also lived in the back of their store. During the fire, Mrs. Hanson and Mrs. Carl Hanson (a friend, no relation) had a lot of adrenaline flowing. They carried all of the furniture out of the Roy Hanson's apartment and put it in a metal building Roy had. It took a lot more people to put it back in place after the fire was extinguished.

I owed the lumberyard for some lumber I had purchased from them, so they filed a claim with their insurance company. The insurance company paid them $335. I had the hole fixed for $35. I never fixed the ceiling, so the remaining $300 went toward my note with the lumberyard.

From a farmer, I bought a box that fit in the back of my 1929 Chev coupe which made a small pickup out of it. I'd go out about sundown when it started cooling off, butcher an animal, and leave it hanging overnight. I had some eight foot 2x6 boards that I bolted together when I got ready to butcher and hang the beef up. I'd leave it until morning. Then I went out early before the flies got around, and brought it to town. I had built the ice cooler by this time. Sometimes it was quite a struggle to hang the fresh meat up. I took beef on grocery bills which was a help to a lot of people.

Louis, William, Lydia, Walter, Henry Sr., Melvin, Henry Jr.

Henry August with his Grandchildren,
1936

One day in the spring of 1936, a brown-eyed, dark-haired girl came to the restaurant in Richland to work. Before long we decided to form a partnership when we decided to get married. When we picked the day, just at random, we picked the last day in October forgetting it was Halloween. So that is our anniversary. I married Velma Belle Draper on October 31, 1936. I was to meet Velma at her parents' home south of Glentana at 11A.M. We would drive over to Scobey, get married, then go down to Glasgow to visit her sister, Iva, for a while, and then back to Richland.

One of the ranchers in the area owed me $53, which was a lot of money in those days. I was to get a beef from him. I got up early in the morning of our wedding day, and took off to butcher this beef as he was moving his cattle to western Montana for the winter. They had already started to move the cattle when I got to the ranch, about twenty miles out of town. I had to go after them and get my beef, which I did. I was a little late for my 11A.M. appointment. Velma always said I took a cow ahead of her on her wedding day. It was late when we got back to Richland. The upstairs above the store was full of people. I had said nothing to my family but somebody got wind of it and let them know. And of course, Velma's folks were there. My Dad was there singing "Where is My Wandering Boy Tonight?". I guess he kept them entertained. The town had a dance all set up. They took up a collection which came to $80, a lot of money in the mid-thirties. I don't know what we bought with it, but I imagine there were a lot of things Velma needed. She helped me in the store. I think over the years Velma did a lot of worrying, especially when I had to go farther than I planned, or if I had to wait. We had no eight to five, just the other way, five to eight, if lucky.

Melvin and Velma, 1937

Velma said she had too much competition. Her mother brought down a loaf of fresh bread. Then the neighbor brought one over. Maybe Velma didn't have an oven. I don't remember what I had in the apartment. She baked a pan of cinnamon rolls when Walter and his family came to visit. She watched the store while we went up to eat. Later she said, "You ate them all. I never got any." I guess she was right.

I used to go out in the pasture to shoot the steers. If there was a bull around you would kind of wonder what sort of mood he might be in. I went to Ray Varsnik's one night after dark. Ray knew what animal he wanted butchered; and managed, in the dark, to shoot it. There was a bull in the herd that I did not know about. He never bothered us. The next day I was out to Jack Skelly's to butcher an animal in the same herd. Jack was helping me. He was scared to death of that bull, although it was a quarter mile away. He skinned and kept looking and said, "If he comes, I'm going." I laughed till I couldn't work. It was no laughing matter to Jack. He'd been chased by a bull once when he was on horseback. He said every jump the horse made, the bull was right behind him giving him a bump. Somehow he beat the bull to the barn.

What worried me was when I had to butcher a steer out in the pasture. If you missed and he did not like it, you had nowhere to go with the time you had. I was lucky, I guess. I never missed.

1937

Rosalie was born on September 30, 1937. She married Johnie Holding on July 9, 1960. They have one daughter, Lisa, born August 26, 1972.

1938

Rosalie had the whooping cough when she was a baby. We made a mixture of honey and something else that we would give her. I'd have to get up in the night to keep her from choking. It was a long six months.

1939

Shorty, who stayed at the hotel, would come over and take Rosalie over to the Restaurant to buy her an ice cream cone. This meant a cleanup job when she got home.

In 1939 the Farmers' Union got the idea that they wanted to start some stores, and wanted to buy us out. As we had gotten through the rough times, we did not want to sell; but there wasn't room in that small town for more than one grocery store. They would have opened one in competition to us, so we sold. The government had a deal where each one could get – I don't remember - $36 or $50 shares, which would go into a co-op fund for a store. I told the Farmers' Union if they could sell enough shares to buy me out at the price we had agreed on, I would sell. They traveled the county over and, in some cases, did a little lying, but couldn't sell enough. They were

$600 short, but we sold to them anyway, and gave them a year to pay off the balance. I think it was one of my mistakes that I sold out. When the Farmers' Union took over the store, they brought in a manager from St. Paul. He was an eight to five man, no twenty-four hour job for him. The store kept shorter hours, and never handled fresh meat. It was a failure. I also regret taking Velma away from her family and taking the grandchildren away from the grandparents who enjoyed them. I should have given this some thought then, not sixty years later.

I had gotten a seed loan for $150 from the government in 1931. It was past due in 1939. The man in charge of the local office said I had to pay the loan off in full, because government money was financing the sale of the store. There would be no deal unless I did. He was a little late getting to our meeting, and by the time he got there I had the money from the sale. He didn't know what to say or do as he had no say over the deal anyway. The Farmers' Union was to make a payment on the store of $100 the next year. I told him to figure the interest I owed to the time the money was due, and have the total due come to $100. I would pay him the rest right away. The next year I got a notice that I was short eight or nine dollars on the payment. I wrote and told them they had figured it and it should be right. The Spokane office sent a correction saying I owed two or three dollars, which I paid. Later, when we made a trip back home, the loan officer caught me in Richland and wanted the money. He didn't know I had paid it. I gave him a bad time for a while and finally told him I didn't owe it. He said, "Oh, you know how it is, a little over or under, just goes in a kitty." It looked to me it just went in for someone else.

About the time we sold out they had arrested a bank robber and had him in jail in Glasgow. There was a sky light in the roof of his cell and some way he managed to squeeze through and get away. We had no bank in Richland. The Farmers' Union oil station usually kept quite a lot of cash on hand for change, and to cash checks. The robber had made the remark that he was going to Richland to rob the station as they had quite a bit of money there. Maybe he said this before he was arrested; but we were concerned about it when he got out. We had finished taking inventory of the store and went over to the restaurant to eat, leaving my nieces Esther and Audrey at the store. When we got back, luckily someone spoke and they recognized us. Those two little girls were ready to blast away with my pistol. They had the robber on their minds, I guess.

We stayed with the Drapers over Christmas.

Oregon
1940's

We had a few leads from salesmen on stores for sale. One was in Loma, Montana. It didn't look too good. Loma is on the river, and no one could cross at that spot because there was no bridge there. So we went on to another town, but the store for sale did not have the post office. The post office was in a competitor's store. We went on to Cut Bank. The store there seemed all right. The price was okay, although we did not have enough money. But the people who traded there had money and could not be bothered with a grocery bill under $500. So it was no good for us, and we loaded our few belongings in our 1938 International pickup and took off west. We stored our furniture at a friend's place.

We just about got blowed off the road at Browning. The wind was terrible. A man told me, "You never need to haul garbage. Put it out at night and in the morning it's gone."

We stopped in Spokane and met a former neighbor from out by the farm. He was looking for a lost gold mine. I went with him a day or two, as he had no way to get around. Then we went on. A few weeks later someone did find the mine. According to the story, one man killed his partner and took off, which seems to be the case.

We left Spokane and got to The Dalles and stayed over night. In those days we traveled the old Columbia River Highway. It's a crooked road. It took us most all day to get to Portland. We were headed for the World's Fair in California, but money goes fast; and I thought we should find something to bring some in as there were no jobs to be had.

Melvin at the Portland Market

We bought a market, mostly fruit stand, on 96th SE Stark, on twenty acres of land we had to rent in order to get the corner the market sat on. But the rent was less than $600 a year, so not too bad. We rented some rooms in an old house until we could fix up a place to live on the end of the building we bought. We ran a partition through one end with plywood. We had a little airtight heater for heat, and gas to cook on. To get gas for heat they wanted a $20 deposit and we had to deposit $60 with the electric company. I'd never pay the electric bill 'till it got close to $60. They complained, but I told them, "You got my $60. When you refund that, I'll keep it paid up." The gas company didn't get my business as I just got the little heater and used it.

Things were bad. The small stores would go and buy part cases of groceries from large chain stores like Safeway, which wasn't the way we had been buying. We finally decided to go down town to the grocery wholesalers. A man by the name of Maynard had a small store on Division. He would come to our store every day and buy a can or two of whatever he was low on. We gave it to him at our cost.

And, of course, again we gave credit. But we managed. Then Albers Feed Mill talked us into stocking some feed, which was something new again.

In 1941 the war came on and things picked up. But then we had the ration stamps. This was almost worse than running on short money. Prices were frozen. Each stamp was worth a certain number of points, and each item was marked with the number of points it cost the consumer. The stores had to send in points in order to get merchandise. Points were more important than money. People often traded stamps. If one person had stamps for an item they didn't need, but someone else could use, they would swap. The value of the stamps was changed every few days, and you'd spend most of the night taking inventory and changing your tags.

During the war I worked in the St. John Shipyard which was about twenty miles from where we lived. After the yard got going, they ran a bus from Estacada to the yard. I caught the bus on 82nd Street. Jim Reese, a colored man, rode the bus with me. He would say, "Let's sit a spell." I'd tell him that we had better get our clothes and be ready for the bus. Once or twice on my days off Jim sat a spell and went to sleep and didn't get to work.

In the beginning of the shipyards, the union wouldn't take on any more members. They were afraid that the members they had might get bumped out of jobs if they did. So they charged the workers a dollar a day for the privilege of working. By the time I was applying for a job they were taking members again. It cost me $40 to join. I paid my dues at the union headquarters, where I was given a number; then went down to the union hall to wait. It was a big barn-like building where everyone came to wait for their number to be called. There were thousands of applicants. It seemed like it should take a long time to get down the list, but it really didn't. If you weren't there when they called your number, no job. I waited three days; then I had a job.

I started out working days. It was an inside job. I should have stayed where I was, but I wanted swing shift so that I could help out in the store during the day and do the purchasing of merchandise. I was switched to swing shift and ended up working outside in the rain. I was always sick. I helped build the seven-day ships (ships that were built in seven days).

One of our grocery customers worked in one of the old shipyards down town just a couple of miles from home. He told me they were hiring and if I could get a job there, I could ride to work with him. I went down to union headquarters. There were three windows there where we paid our dues. At that time they still collected locally. From there I went to the business office. I went up to the business office window. I was at the head of the line. The guard told me the business agent wasn't in and would not be in until after lunch at one o'clock. After lunch the guard said the agent wasn't in and wouldn't be in until later. I told him it was funny that we could have three windows to take our money, but couldn't have one for a business agent. He told me again he'd be in later in the afternoon. I told him I couldn't wait as I had to go to work on the swing shift. He said, "What are you complaining about? You have a job." I worked at the shipyard for fourteen months as a welder. Then I quit. I was chronically ill from the wet weather.

While I was working at the shipyard, Velma ran the store, with some help. I would be there in the morning some, as I worked swing shift.

During the war a man came to me and wanted me to buy a calf from him. He had bought it thinking he had plenty of grass in his back yard to feed it. The grass ran out pretty quick. We had quite a bit of grass so I took it and raised it. She was a good milk cow, not too much milk, but really rich. We had some calves from her too. We butchered them until the last one. She was such a pretty thing I sure hated to take her to the stockyard, but as we were leaving I had to. I sold the cow to a "cow trader," a man who bought and sold cows.

There was a man going into the armed service who had a pig and little ones. He wanted me to buy them. This was too much for me. I didn't want to mess with pigs. Charlie Williams, one of my colored customers, said if I would buy the pigs, he would raise them and we would split the money. He was to get our vegetable waste to feed the pigs and would also purchase some of the feed we sold at the store. As they got big enough, he'd butcher them and we would share. He sold all of these pigs. Then I bought a big pig that weighed about 175 pounds. Charlie kept it a little while and butchered it out. He kept half the pig, which shorted me in the deal.

Somewhere around the year 1943, Fred and Violet McCarty came back to Portland. Fred was a very stubborn man. He was in the service and didn't want to be there. He did everything he could think of to get out. They had a gas drill. I guess they didn't tell him to put his gas mask on so he went in without it. Another time they were on the firing range. Someone said, "Fire," and Fred fired. There were still some men on the range who could have been hit. He told them, "You said, 'Fire.'" They finally discharged him.

Velma	Melba	Rosalie	Corinne	Melvin
		1944		

The McCartys had an old car and trailer, and they told us to use it and take a couple weeks to go back to Montana. They would take care of the store. Violet had worked for us before. It seemed like a good deal, so Velma packed a lunch and we took off. The trailer was just a box on the frame, no springs. That lunch was just one big mess. The salt and pepper shakers were broken up and everything was all mixed together. All of the food had to be thrown out. Coming down the hill into Cut Bank, Montana, just as it was getting dark, we lost a wheel off the trailer. We looked that brush over in the half-dark, found it, got it back on the trailer, and went into Cut Bank. We stayed over night and got our wheel taken care of the next morning. It was pretty hot out by the time we got going, and before we got very far out of town that old car vapor locked. I hadn't had any experience with vapor lock and didn't know what to do. I guess someone poured some cold water on it or something and got it going. We got to Scobey.

The gas situation on that trip was interesting. I just had ration stamps for a pickup, because we didn't have a car. The McCartys had a few extra stamps which they gave us. We got to Scobey on those.

Hank had a lot of gasoline as he was farming quite a bit of land. He had a diesel tractor which seemed to be something the government didn't know how to deal with. As far as they were concerned he needed so much gas to farm with and that was it. He got the gas they thought he needed, even though he didn't need it. We filled a bunch of cans for the trip home, and got home on that gas.

On the way home the old car vapor locked again going through Missoula, Montana; but I managed to keep it going and it took us back to Portland.

Our lease ran out in 1945. They were going to give us a couple more years, but a competitor in the feed business down the street bought the land. It was a mistake not looking into buying it. It was an estate and one of the heirs was in a mental home, which tied it up. This woman died which opened it up to be sold.

We were lucky to get a piece of property on 122nd and Division, almost a quarter block except for the corner on which a small grocery store stood. A young man had built a building on the property with the intention of starting a feed store there, but he didn't have the money to stock it so became discouraged and offered to sell it to us. We started a feed store there.

There was just one building on the property with no place to store hay, so I had a man help me build a shed for hay. I had foundation frames run and had them filled in to make the foundation truck-bed high. I cut the walls of the building we had on 96th and Stark into sections. The section we had been living in was moved out to the two and one-half acres we had purchased on 148th and Stark; and was where we lived after that. Bill thought he was going to have a summer job tearing the remaining walls apart and rebuilding them for the feed store. When I told him we were just going to set them up as they were, he said, "A twenty-five dollar building an a thousand dollar foundation."

We couldn't get feed from Albers because they said we were too close to their dealer in Lentz. We were no closer to Lentz than we had been in our other location, but I suppose they did have customers in that area. Feed was short, but Triangle Feed said they would give us what they could spare, so we had a limited stock. But it picked up, and a year later we had a good stock of feed and a nice business built up.

We had a man bring us in oat and vetch hay. It seemed we were always short as it was weighed when we sold it. Come to find out, the scale tickets he brought were just some he had filled out without weighing.

86

There wasn't too much money in the feed business. About 5% profit. If we sold a sack of feed for six dollars, we would get thirty cents. That was the way the feed mills had it set up then. If we delivered, we charged a nickel more.

Then my good friend, Harry Truman, then president, cut us back to eighty percent of what stock we had the year before, plus cutting out a number of feeds. We were back worse than we had been before. We sold the business and buildings on our acreage and moved back to Montana. The man I sold out to in 1947 wrote and said he made five hundred dollars that first year. Of course, he was short on stock, as the war, the Marshall Plan, and the low feed quota the store had, made feed hard to get.

I could have made a fortune if I had kept what I had and just went to work some place. And I had a chance to buy more. One piece of ground, about ten acres, was offered to me for six thousand dollars. I said I didn't have the money. The man said I didn't need money, but I didn't move on the deal. In two weeks developers bought it for eighteen thousand dollars.

A man who had a wrecking yard down the street from us ran into the same thing we did. He was just leasing, and some developer bought it. He had to move. I was told that lots on our two and one-half acre plot later sold for twenty-nine thousand dollars. I don't know how true that was, but that's water under the bridge.

In the summer of 1946, before I sold out, I hauled quite a lot of wheat from Eastern Oregon which I bought from farmers. I was told a man up in Hereford, Oregon, up in the John Day country, had some hay he wanted to sell, and the price was right. Early one morning I took off for Hereford. I got there about three in the afternoon, had something to eat, and got directions how to get to his place. He had hay, about fifteen hundred tons, but not baled, just loose stacked. It was too much hay for me and I wasn't prepared to bale it anyway. He said he didn't want me to go back empty, so he would help me get some wheat. He called a neighbor who was to meet us at their gate. A woman and a boy met us. The rancher who had come with me wasn't too well, but we started loading anyway. The wheat was in sacks, 120 to 140 pounds each. They had one of those hanging scales. It was almost impossible to hold a sack of wheat up there, get it hooked, and then balance it. We put ten sacks on the truck and I asked the lady to average them out and use that for a figure so we would not have to weigh any more. She said she didn't think her husband would like that. We put on a few more sacks and gave up. I did not go back to Hereford, and after I was on the road a ways, got to thinking about gas. Studying the map, it looked like there might be a town a little way up the road toward home, so I turned up this road. The road was new, under construction. I couldn't see any place to get gas, so started to turn around. I got a little too far out on the new shoulder. The back end went down and off goes my wheat. This happened near a road camp. Luckily, a couple of men came along in a truck, pulled me out, and helped me to get loaded again. They said the town I was looking for was one or two miles farther on. I asked them what I owed them for their help. They said, "Nothing. You're in Eastern Oregon now." I went back to John Day, filled up with gas and bought enough cans of gas to get me back home. I had a flat tire and got home about ten the next morning. Mrs. Earl, a friend, met me at the door. Velma wasn't there. She was in the hospital. Karen had surprised us and had arrived early.

We had three more girls born into our family while we lived in Portland. Corinne was born on May 18, 1940. She married Dexter Miles on December 30, 1962. They have five children:

Darrell – born October 5, 1963

Craig – born December 1, 1964

Carla – born February 16, 1966

Michele – born December 24, 1967

Andrea - born October 23, 1977

Melba was born in Portland, Oregon on November 18, 1943. She married Clair Folckomer on June 10, 1962. They have three children:

Nadine – born August 1, 1964

Bradley – born July 25, 1970

Gregory – born March 2, 1972

Karen was born in Portland, Oregon on October 15, 1946. She married Ed Bernier on August 16, 1967. They have two girls:

Sherri – born April 16, 1968

Janice – born October 30, 1970

Another time I went to Spray to get some wheat. Velma and girls went along with me. We stopped on the way and had a picnic lunch, got our wheat, and started back. Corinne and Rosalie were in the back. We got down to the river and it started to rain. The girls sat on the wheat under the tarp. The truck started acting up. We finally got to Lookout Point when it quit. I had to walk several miles in the rain to a station. I got what I needed for the fuel pump, got it going and got home around noon the second day. It seems things were pretty wet there as I was putting a new roof on the building.

Scobey, Montana

After we sold the feed store, we went to Scobey, Montana, and purchased a dray and coal business. We left the three younger girls in Malta with Iva, Velma's sister, and took Rosalie with us back to Portland to help pack up our belongings. I traded the pickup for a four-cylinder truck. We loaded everything we could on the truck, left a few things to be sold at the local auction, and took off. We crossed the Columbia River to Vancouver and drove down the Washington side of the river because the road was not so crooked as the Oregon side. We got down the road a piece to White Salmon, across the river from Hood River, and had to put in gas. I hoped the fuel tank was small. It turned out to be a twenty-gallon tank. We made five miles to the gallon on the way to Spokane. We had started down the mountain into Wallace, Idaho, when a bread truck waved us down. A tire had gone bad. We had spares, but by the time we got all through, we were short two tires. This was 1947 and getting tires was not that easy.

We took off one tire on each side of the back of the truck, where there should have been two on each side. We drove slowly, about twenty-five miles an hour. Late that night we stopped and got a cabin at St. Regis, Montana. Next morning we found a place where we could buy one tire. I had not prepared for all the extra gas and expenses, but they took a check for seventy dollars for part of the cost of the tire. We put the new tire on one side and the two old ones on the other side.

We rolled right along until we got to Loma, Montana. There is a long hill there, and when I tried to shift the gears, they stuck. It had started to rain and was dark. I caught a ride back to Loma and, in time, found a man who would go out and look at the truck. The problem was that the people who owned the truck before we did had put too light a grease in it. Driving it hard, as I was doing, caused the transmission to get too warm. By the time we got back to the truck and took the cover off the gear case, we were able to get the gears to move. The mechanic told me I would have to take it to town, take it apart, and sand the driveshaft down, as the gears were too tight. I told him to put it in low gear and I would bypass second and go to high. That worked. We went all the way to Malta in third gear. We drove through the night. Our greatest obstacle was a flock of sheep we had to maneuver through at Havre. We went through Havre at daybreak.

89

We got to Malta where Iva lived. I let Velma and Rosalie off and said, "I'm going to drive around the block and see if I can shift now." It worked fine. No more gear trouble.

We stayed in Malta three days. Velma had gotten sick before we left Portland, and was still pretty sick when we got to Malta. She spent those three days in the old house they used for a hospital there. The doctor and hospital together cost fourteen dollars.

When we got to Scobey there were three cars of coal waiting to be unloaded. We also had to find a place to live. We did find a house to rent; and with help from Walter's oldest son, Harold Siggelkow, and some others, we got the coal unloaded. We unloaded twenty-two cars of coal in forty days, all by hand.

Along about February, the people who were collecting our house rent told us the owners were planning to move back to Scobey, and we would have to move from there. At that time there were no houses available. We bought a lot and an old house to move on to it. That house had a history. It had been a bootlegger's house in the old days. It was called the Dirty Shame because it had been built between two other moonshine establishments, the owners of which thought it was a dirty shame that a competitor had moved into the neighborhood. The Dirty Shame was in the business more seriously than it's neighbors were. It had card games and moonshine. The Miller boys lost their flax crop there. The house was fixed up with a trap door over a well where the booze could be quickly disposed of in case of a raid. They had time to do this because they had an extra heavy door on the house that was not easy to break in. The door was hauled to Great Falls as evidence in the trial when the authorities were finally able to catch the bootleggers. Each of them got a year in jail.

I had a basement dug and started to build a house. I didn't get it done in time to move in by winter, and it got real cold the next winter; so we moved into the basement to live for the winter. We fixed up one room at a time starting with the kitchen, and slowly got moved up into the house proper.

| Melba | Rosalie | Corinne | Karen |

Everything moved along kind of quiet. I bought a small Ferguson tractor with a scoop, so we did not have to shovel all the coal by hand. I also had an auger made to auger the stoker coal into the bins. I bought an old single-axle trailer that was in bad shape and put it on the old International truck that had come with the business.

One day I started off for Lewistown, Montana. The old International had a hard time pulling the trailer. I hadn't used the truck much and didn't look things over very well. I got about sixty-five miles down the road and the water pump started leaking. I went into a farmer's yard. No one was home and I couldn't find a grease gun, so I went down the road to another farm and got one. I was on the road again. I got down into the Jordan country. When I went to shift, I got my wires in a tangle and the truck lights went out. I stopped and went to sleep until daylight, which came early in mid-summer. I got up and went on to Lewistown, about three hundred ten miles from home. I got there about 10A.M. I went out to the sheetrock plant, another ten miles. I didn't stop to eat, as I thought I'd load first. I had to wait until three or four in the afternoon to load, got one half load of sheetrock, hurried back to Lewistown to the brick yard, got the other half load in brick, ate, and started home. That old International truck didn't have the get-up-and-go it needed. It took a long time to make some of those hills. Most of the time you could walk faster than the truck moved with that load.

Some years later one of my hired men was with me when we were hauling a load of coal going up a long hill. (Normally, the coal would be shipped by rail, but sometimes in the spring of the year when the supply was getting low, I would haul a truckload from Roundup. Sometimes there might be a rail strike or a mine strike and I would go to Westby for a truckload to tide us over.) I made some comment, and he said, "Yes, and we are going awful slow." We got over by the Musselshell River, and coming out of there the old truck said, "These hills are too much!" But, by jerks and jumps, we made it keep going until we got over about thirty-five miles east of Jordan, and there we had a flat tire. I caught a ride into Circle where a friend of mine lived. He took me back out the thirty miles to the truck, and we took the tire in to Brockway, had it fixed, and I was on my way again. When we later got the truck into Circle, I discovered that a wheel on the semi-trailer had been run loose and the nuts were bad. They would not stay tight. There was nothing to do but try to get home, stopping every few miles to tighten the wheel. It took all day to get home. The trip took two days and two nights. I had a lot of fun with that outfit. That old International truck just wasn't up to hauling a semi, and I had a lot of trips that were rather bad. Dale, one of my hired men, called the outfit, Betsy and Her Bustle.

In 1952 I bought a three-cylinder Jimmy, a GMC diesel truck, not too powerful and not too fast; but I hauled a lot of sheetrock and other things with it. Until that time I was still using the old International two-ton that came with the dray business. On my first trip with the Jimmy, I went to Washington with a load of furniture. I got to Coeur d'Alene, Idaho, where the scale was. The scaleman looked at my ragged outfit and was about to let me go, when he said, "Will you be coming back this way?" I said I was, so he said, "I'll have to charge you." He put some stickers on my windshield and charged me five dollars. I went on to Ritzville, Washington. I thought I'd better get some fuel as I had not put any in since leaving home, which would be about eight hundred fifty miles. I had two forty-gallon tanks, which I later found out would go for sixteen hours. I pulled into a station. A man came out to wait on me, and I went into the rest room. When I came out he said, ""Have you a Washington fuel permit?" I didn't. "I can't sell you any fuel," he said. He finally gave me twenty gallons on his own account. I went on to Ephrata. I got there about noon and the house wasn't ready to put furniture in. I waited around for the carpenters to get a floor down so I could unload, and I thought, "I need fuel." I drank coffee to while the afternoon away. About dark I got unloaded and a dealer came to bring me fuel. My tanks could not hold fifty gallons, so he had to charge the fuel to himself. As a bulk dealer he could not sell less, I guess. I paid him cash for the fuel. I tried to sleep, but all that coffee was too much. Finally I got up and left for home. I had gone a short way and saw some loose paper in the box was blowing out, so I pulled over to the edge of the paved road. When I went to go again, my outside wheels were in the sand and I could not go. I finally found myself in an Eastern Washington wheat field. I got a down hill shot and got back on the road. I by-passed the scale and got over into the Idaho mountains. Then I pulled over and went to sleep. I awoke and went on to Montana, near Kalispell, and went to sleep again. In the morning I went on to Columbia Falls and got a load of lumber. I had no permit for that trip or for many others later. I got home and filled the truck with fuel. That diesel had made twelve miles to the gallon.

I decided I had better get some permits for hauling. I had a local attorney, Fosland, make out the papers for MRC (Montana Railroad Commission) permits to haul sheetrock from Lewistown and farm implements from Billings and various other places where I had been picking things up for some of the local dealers. The first time the attorney made a mistake in the forms so he had to redo them. He had me sign the papers for him to fill out later. He neglected to specify all the towns I wanted; so my permit read Lewistown to Scobey, Billings to Scobey, no towns in between. It was a limited permit to these cities along with a fifty mile radius from Scobey. I still ended up doing a lot of illegal driving. I moved a lot of people's furniture over the years, and never got caught. Lucky, I guess.

To get a MRC permit to haul (They were called a convenience and necessity permit.) you should have four business people who needed this service. Well, Vic Hillstrom, Hellickson Lumber, the other lumber yard, and H. P. Larson Implement all said they would back me to get it. When my hearing date came it seemed no one had time. Vic Hillstrom, a car dealer, went with me to Culbertson, sixty-five miles from home. My attorney thought his services weren't needed there, so he didn't go. I couldn't do anything with what I had to work with, but the commissioner said he'd give me another hearing date. My next hearing was in Great Falls, four hundred miles away. There was another trucker in town, Charlie Harris, who did contract work, so no one wanted to testify for me. They were afraid of offending Charlie. People were willing to give me affidavits, but would not show up in person. Vic Hillstrom again said that one of the people in his business would go. The Hellickson Lumber manager asked me if I was ready to go. I told him I wasn't going. He wanted to know why. I told him I'd been there once without the witnesses I needed. No more. He said he would let Harold Slater go to represent their business. Jim Hillstrom went to represent another lumberyard. Walt Vanderpan, working for the other yard, was taking inventory in Malta but would be through. I called him and as he finally ran out of excuses, he had to come out and say, "I don't think I should," meaning he did not want to offend my competition who did some business with him. My attorney made arrangements with an attorney friend of his in Great Falls to represent me. This attorney was part of a firm in which there was a man with some experience in this line. I got a good attorney. "We can try," he said, "but it doesn't look too good. We need more witnesses." I called Marvin Sorte who worked for Pete Larson, an implement and lumber dealer. He was through with the job he was on and could catch the train and be in Great Falls in time for the hearing. He was to call back in two hours. He called back and said Pete wouldn't let him come for the same reason Walt wouldn't go. The attorney was not too happy, but he said, "You're here. We might as well try. Maybe we can get in on the late hearing, and they might be in a hurry to get through and overlook our shortage." This proved to be the case as it was around 7P.M. before we got through. After the hearing the lawyers wanted to go in one of the swanky hotels to have a drink or two. To get out of there, we said we wanted to get something to eat. They said, "You can eat right here." Well, what could we do but stay. We looked the menu over and the cheapest thing was a chicken sandwich for $2.50. Today (1994) that wouldn't be high, but this was 1953. The boys knew I didn't have too much money to waste on this trip so we all ordered chicken sandwiches, which we ate. The waitress said, "You were hungry enough to eat it all after all."

I got involved in buying scrap iron about this time. Here's how it happened: One of the men in the area had some trouble with his wife and left her, took a tractor about twenty miles out of town to Wesley Howard's place, and hid it. The family found it and had me haul it back to town. While I was at Wesley's he talked me into buying a big old Rumley tractor he had. I tore it down and hauled it to town. There never was any money in selling scrap iron, but if you could bring a load of something back it helped pay expenses. I hauled a lot of scrap over the next fifteen years.

After I got started in the scrap iron business, I hauled a lot to Minnesota when I could get a load to haul back. I must have crossed North Dakota one hundred times without paying a road tax. One of my last trips with iron I went to Williston. By the time I got unloaded it was getting late in the afternoon. As it was the sixteenth of December, the days were short. It started to storm and get cold, but I knew if I stayed overnight that diesel truck wouldn't start. So I took off. I got to Culbertson. The visibility was bad but I got to Plentywood. It was thick in town, but not too bad outside. So I went on. I got about three miles from Flaxville and hit a dust/snowstorm. I put on my brakes to stop and let it clear. I did not know there was ice. My trailer jack-knifed on me and I was stuck. I got out to put chains on. It was thirty below with a strong wind. A man came along and waited to see if I could get going. I got the chains on and got on the road again. It was so cold in the cab I could not get my windshield to clear off, so I drove to Flaxville with my head out of the window. I was too cold to go farther, so I pulled the truck off to the side and got a room. There were two other trucks there. It was so cold their fuel froze up. It took them all the next day to get the trucks inside and thawed out. My fuel was number one and had a continuous flow, so at least I did not have that happen. I caught a ride home with a fuel truck the next day. Over the years I hauled a lot of furniture, sheetrock, and scrap iron; and had a lot of fun, and also some worries.

My brother, Bill, had cancer, from which he died in 1959. He lived in Saskatchewan, Canada, where they tell me the health system is so good. They treated him for a heart condition, and when they finally decided he had cancer it was too late. About a year before he died he went with me to Minneapolis with a load. I carried enough fuel for sixteen hours of driving, and he was worried about me not stopping for fuel.

After that trip, Bill decided he was going to the West Coast with me. I had a Chev cab-over two-ton truck I'd bought, a used one. I took it up to a local mechanic and told him to check the brakes, generator and other things; as I was taking this truck with a load of furniture to Battle Ground, just north of Vancouver, Washington. It was the first part of November and cold, about twenty-five below. We loaded up and got away late in the day. We got to Malta, where Velma's sister, Iva, lived. We stopped and had a cup of coffee, and left there about sundown. Our lights seemed awfully dim, so we stopped in Chinook to see what was wrong. Our generator wasn't working. The man there ran a little sandpaper over it and got it working. We went on to Havre and got a bed. We got up the next morning and found the generator had quit again. As we did not need lights, we went on till evening and got to Sandpoint, Idaho. The man at the station didn't have time to help us, so I got a piece of sandpaper and got the generator going. We drove late into the night to Ritzville, Washington, and went to bed.

The next morning, no generator. We drove on to Pasco and over to Kennewick, where we hit a dense fog. We got turned around and parked the truck and went to find a garage. We found one. They put in one brush and got us going. We went across the Columbia River at Umatilla and drove down the Oregon side of the river. The wind was blowing hard and the tarp was flapping. I couldn't see too good through my rear view mirror. A state patrolman stopped me near Arlington which was a central point for them at that time. He mentioned that my view wasn't too good as I had not seen his lights flashing. He asked some questions. I said as little as I needed to about what I was doing. Then he said, "You haul a little furniture sometimes?" Of course, I had to admit to that, but he let me go. We got into Battle Ground late, after dark. Bill looked out across the valley and said, "How are you going to find anything in all this?"

We drove on into town, stopped to check, and did not have an address. They had put their address on the boxes, so I had to get in the load to find it. We were only two blocks from the house. We went up and unloaded our load and went back to Vancouver to bed. We got up the next morning and went on to Portland as we had a couple of nieces there. I asked Audrey if she knew a good mechanic where I could get my generator fixed. She did, and for twenty-five dollars I got a couple more brushes put in. It all seemed pretty good now for the trip home.

I was to pick up a small load of lumber at the Weyerhaeuser Mill over in Washington. So, early in the morning we took off. We got to the mill and had to wait. There was no place there to eat; and Bill with his cancer couldn't eat much at a time, but had to eat more often. About 4 P.M. we got loaded and started back for the highway. I was hurrying along, trying to beat the evening rush, when the truck stopped. We were lucky. There was a bus turn-off and we could get off the road. Then it started raining and began to get dark. I couldn't get the truck to go. I went on foot to a gas station and got some distributor points. It was dark and raining. What can you do? One of the coil wires was pretty well frayed out. Finally, I told Bill, "If it don't start now we'll have to give up." It started. We got down the road a ways and found a place to eat. It was now 8 P.M. We drove on to Arlington and went to bed.

The next day we kept going. As we were coming into Spokane, I stepped on the brake. No action. I let the truck coast on through Spokane before I stopped to have it checked. The brake cylinder was full of oil and just needed pumping a few times. This was fine and we went on our way. As we came to a long hill by Hot Springs, Montana, I pumped the brakes, but no brakes. The hill is about five miles long, and when you get to the bottom there is a stop sign for a highway intersection. Nothing to do but let it roll, and fortunately, no one was coming on the highway. We went on until the truck stopped, and we shifted down to low gear. We found a service station that was open and got a can of brake fluid. We went on to Kalispell. The next morning we took the truck to a garage, and by afternoon they had our brakes fixed. We were on our way again. We were fifty-five dollars poorer. About three o'clock the next morning we got home. Bill said he'd never be a trucker for all the money in the world.

The garage that had supposedly checked over my truck seemed to think all was well. At least I never got a refund.

Louie, Walter, Hank, Melvin, & Lydia at Bill's Funeral

Over the years I was in a lot of odd situations. One time a teenager who had been working on the farms around Scobey wanted to ride to Minneapolis with me as I was hauling a load of scrap iron to Minnesota. For some reason I felt uneasy about taking him. I told him I would be stopping in St. Cloud, Minnesota, to unload, and would go straight south and bypass Minneapolis. He said that was fine. He'd catch a ride from St. Cloud. I still didn't feel right about giving him a ride, so I got up at 3:00 A.M. to take off and leave him, but he was sitting in the truck waiting. He had a bundle of loose clothes with him, so I went into the house and got a sack to put them in. Later, when I was ready to leave, I saw that he had put a guitar in the sack and had stuck the clothes in the load of iron. We made it to Mahnomen, Minnesota, that day. I got two rooms. I was carrying quite a lot of money with me because I was going to Indiana for building supplies. We got to St. Cloud that day and got unloaded. Then he decided to go on to southern Minnesota with me because he could get a ride to where he wanted to go from there. When we got to southern Minnesota he thought he'd better go farther on with me, as he wanted to go north of Chicago somewhere. We went to Council Bluffs, Iowa, where Velma's brother, Lloyd, lived. I told him this was the end of the line because I would be staying with my brother-in-law and could not bring in a stranger. I got a piece of rope and bundled up his loose clothes and he left me.

Lloyd was remodeling his house, so I went on. I slept in the truck a while, and went on to Terre Haute, Indiana. I got there early in the morning and was told I would have to wait to get loaded. I did. I waited all day and half the night until three the next morning. When I finally got my load, I took off and drove to Rock Island, Illinois. After I got across the line I felt better. I had been told the ICC (Interstate Commerce Commission) checked pretty close there, but I passed their inspection, got over and bought fuel. I was so tired I found a place to park the truck and went to sleep. I got home with my load. I was told the young man who had ridden with me had stolen the clothes he was wearing, the clothes he was carrying with him, and the guitar from a friend who had given him a place to stay. That long, lean streak of misery also was supposed to be carrying a gun. The sheriff had called the police in Minneapolis to stop me, but I never went there. Had they called the highway patrol they would have done the job. Minnesota has a lot of patrolmen.

I took a load of rabbits down to a mink farm in northern Minnesota. I was also needed to take a load of furniture down to Iowa. A young man in Scobey said he would drive one truck as he wanted to visit his brothers in Minneapolis. When we got down there it was forty degrees below zero and storming some. I got a bed and covered the diesel truck with all the cover I had, as I usually carried some so it wouldn't get too cold to start. I got up several times during the night and started the truck. Early in the morning we went to the mink farm and unloaded the rabbits. We picked up the Chev cab-over and took off for Iowa. We got down to about three miles out of Mahnomen and lost a front wheel off the Chev. We went on into town and found someone to pull us in. By ten the next morning we were on our way. We parked the diesel in Detroit Lakes and went on to Olivia, Minnesota, where I left Kenny and went on to Iowa with my load of furniture. I unloaded and started back. I stopped in southern Minnesota and got a haircut in a small town there. The haircut cost fifty cents. I stopped outside of Minneapolis at what looked like a not-too-bad bus stop, hotel, and restaurant. There was a place to park my truck, so I felt pretty good. I ate and asked about a room. There was one with two beds. One had been occupied and not made up, but I could use the other one. There were whiskey bottles and other debris in the room. Then the racket started. Things got pretty bad. Finally a woman came upstairs and shouted, "If you don't shut up and behave yourselves I'll send you back to St. Cloud." So much for that Saturday night. I went on to Minneapolis and got a room in a motel. It was sure hard to lay over. I met Kenny on Monday morning and went down town to pick up some roofing which, to my knowledge, was all set to go. But they couldn't load me as they could not sell less than ten ton at the factory price. Somebody had goofed. I could not haul over seven or eight tons on the truck I had with me, and I had left the other one in Detroit Lakes. Somehow they arranged to give me a load. They loaded me with what my truck could haul, and by 3:00 P.M. we were on our way. We picked up the other truck and came home.

One time the lumberyard needed some rafters for a barn. A storm had taken the rafters off the barn. I understood I was to pick them up north of Minneapolis. Instead, when the man gave me the order, it was on a mill in Albert Lea. I drove down there and they had no order, and of course, no rafters were ready. There had not been any arrangements for payment made, and it seemed the lumberyard did not have a credit rating with this firm.

They would get busy and make the rafters, but we would have to arrange for the payment. I told them I'd forget it and go home, but they didn't want that. I had a check for my load of iron, larger than the bill would be. I told them I would leave that and they could have their office in Minneapolis send me the difference. They would not agree to that. The next morning they had the rafters and loaded my truck as it was not a big order. Then they asked me to go to the bank and get the money. I knew this didn't make any sense, but I went. The banker said there wasn't anything in it for them, which was true. So I waited. About 10:00 A.M. they said everything is all right, and they would take my personal check. I think if they had contacted Dunn and Bradstreet they could have saved a lot of time, as my credit rating with them was good.

Over all these years I was never stopped by an ICC (Interstate Commerce Commission) man.

1960's

In the meantime I lost the mail contract, and the freight hauling was almost nothing. So I went to work Henry's farm for him. We still sold coal and hauled garbage, but the city decided they wanted to haul the garbage. So there wasn't much left in town for me to do. I let Doug, who had worked for me for many years, go.

I bought a farmhouse south of Flaxville. I had Alfred Bellanger help me to raise it and move it off the foundation and put timbers and wheels under it. The house was plastered and very heavy. We had a bridge to cross, and a power line which had to be taken down about three miles beyond the bridge. The bridge was narrow. We had to raise the building enough to go over the side rails. We calculated wrong and were not high enough to go over the top. Crossing the bridge took more time than we had planned. The crew who had already lowered the power line for us said they'd have to raise it again and go home for the night. We had to find a place to turn off the highway and park for the night. In the process we caught the cold wire on the power line and broke it. It led into a vacant farm, so no harm was done except to have it fixed. The power company sent two men and a big truck with us in the morning. When they got the wire lowered again we were on our way. The men stayed to fix the break. When we got a couple miles onto the gravel road we sank down and were stuck. The house was really leaning. As the house covered the whole road, we had to go about ten miles to get back to the men who were fixing the broken wire. They tied on to us and pulled us out. We got along fine until we got to Scobey. There were several wires that were too low, both telephone and electric. Saturday evening was coming on and the men just could not get all of this work done. The state highway man had been flagging on our back, and he came up and wanted to know what the trouble was. I told him we had a bunch of men here, but nobody was doing anything. Then the telephone man got his spikes and went up the pole. Tom Hagan, the MDU (Montana Dakota Utility) man, had to go to work then, too. Tom had to work a little late, but we got through town and got the house parked and ready for Monday morning. The only bridge we could get over, due to our width, had only six inches clearance. We scraped a little, but got through. The house shifted on the skids and we lost a lot of time getting more blocking and straightening it up. We parked another night. Our power men left us here as we were done with them. I had Alfred Bellanger helping me, and he had a tractor at this spot, so he said to go along and he'd help us with the tractor. We still had several hills and a steep climb out of the creek bottom before we were home.

A little way from the creek we went down in the road again. Al tied on and pulled us out. The bridge was a low water bridge, just eighteen feet wide, on a curve in the road. Hank went across to guide the drivers. Johnie Holding, my son-in-law, was driving the truck pulling the house, and Al was on his tractor. They took off and I tried to keep up on foot as best I could. We had to move our wheels in to come to the eighteen feet, and had no room to spare. We had planned on stopping, getting a straight line and going over slowly. Well, things somehow got mixed up. They came around that curve about twenty miles an hour. Al did not stop. He later said that he thought Hank was waving him on. From my vantage point all I could see was a house tipping over into the creek, but somehow that never happened. They made it across. Just one tire on one side had a few problems getting around a square corner on a country road, but we got the house moved that summer I worked from "see" until "can't see," evenings and mornings in the field; and in the middle of the day, setting forms and pouring cement. But we got moved in.

Corinne's husband, Dexter Miles, decided that he would like to try farming in Montana. He had been working for a successful farmer in Oregon. They moved to Montana in September of 1966.

Years before this all happened, Hank had given financial backing to a man in Fort Peck's grocery store. On paper it looked good, but in a small business, you have to work long hours all the time. After a couple of years he had too much money on his charge accounts and owed too much to the wholesale houses. He gave up and we got a man to take it over. He put $3,000 of his own money in and was going to buy. He worked hard getting bills paid, but after a year he gave up and got his $3000 back from Hank. Melba's husband, Clair Folckomer, did not have a regular job at this time. We got him to move out from Pennsylvania to take it over. He did not have any business training, so pretty soon there was too much credit and not enough stock. He became discouraged, found a job with the telephone company in Seattle, and moved his family out there. We left Dexter and Corinne on the farm and moved to Fort Peck to take over the store operation.

Fort Peck

We put a little money into stocking the store, so we had most everything a person might need. As a service to our customers, we cashed the payroll checks for the dam workers twice a month. To get cash for this we would go to the bank at Glasgow and get $3,000, which cost us a $3 bank fee for two days, until we delivered the checks to the bank. After a short while they said they'd have to have $7. Then they wanted to hold a note in their vault for the $3,000. As it was, we made out a note for each trip. I decided I didn't like that. Then we started buying our merchandise so as to pay for it after pay day, and that eliminated the cost of cashing the checks. No more bank problems.

We were paying a rental of four percent on gross sales, including utilities. Then the engineers decided to put us on a fixed rental average, which came to about $200 a month. When our lease ran out we bid it in at $25 a month. No one bid against us so we got the building for $25. Utilities, including heat, cost $40, so $65 was all we were paying for building expense. We set our prices at a sixteen and two-thirds percent markup, which made us competitive with anyone in the area.

At this time the government built about sixty new homes in Fort Peck, as well as a shopping complex: a café-drug store combination, post office, grocery store, a basement for meetings and a bowling alley. The government was very good to us. We had a good stock and prices were right. They gave us a lot of help in moving and repairing walk-in coolers.

By this time we had a good line of freezers and coolers; but the buildings, like all government buildings, were very poorly planned. The floor was three inches of concrete and the electrical outlets were in the floor. When you wanted an outlet, it was usually under what you wanted it for. We had things all backward, and, of course, the boys did not want to dig in three inches of concrete to change an outlet. One day I told the girls I'd get some action. I turned the checkout stand around and brought the wire over it. We had a small pop cooler we had not been able to use for some time. I brought a long extension cord over the meat counter in the back to the cooler, stuck a 2x1 board up to hold it, and hooked it up. I showed the electrician what I had done. No comment.

We had a bad summer, as there was no way to get a circulation of air through the building. There was no air conditioning. I wanted to put a fan in one corner; but Mr. Kumcheff, the head man, didn't know what that would do to the building, making a hole up there. It was so hot in the store that I'd go down until 11 P.M. and again early in the morning trying to get some cool air into the building. We lost a lot of chocolate candy and other things because the temperature would get to one hundred ten degrees at times.

The next summer, Mr. Beckman, the engineer in charge, came in one day, looked at the extension cord I had strung up and asked what that was. It had been at least a year and a half since I had set it up. Without thinking, I said that was where I hung the diapers to dry. Boy was he mad! He said it would only take one fire at night to burn the whole place down. He had the boys come in after work in overtime to change my cord. I never told him how long it had been that way.

We went to Billings once to an auction sale where a store was closing out, and bought a walk-in cooler. I borrowed a truck to haul it home. I got some men to help me take it apart. I climbed up on top to loosen something that was sticking. The ladder slipped and down I went, eight feet to the ground. After picking myself out of the mess, I found that I had a broken heel and sprained ankle. I called a friend, Harold Carlson, who lived there, and he came to help. The auctioneer helped, too, so we got it apart and loaded. I couldn't drive with only one foot so Harold drove the truck through town and took me to a motel. He brought something for me to soak my foot in, and some bandages. I couldn't sleep, so I got up toward morning, got in the truck and started for home. The truck I was driving did not have an automatic shift. It was a problem with one foot to work clutch, brake and transmission. I got down the road about three miles and the truck quit me, so there I was. Dark. Couldn't walk. Stuck. Some people stopped and took me to a truck stop.

I sat in the truck stop wondering what to do; drank some coffee. Then a couple were getting ready to leave and I asked them if they would take me back to the motel which was not too far from there. It was some distance from the street to the door, and by this time I was having a great deal of difficulty walking. I could not walk all the way and had to crawl part way. The folks who had given me the ride felt bad because they had not realized my condition. I called my friend again and he got a mechanic to bring the truck in and get it running again, then took me to the station where the work was being done so I would be there when the truck was fixed. When the mechanic was through with the truck I took off for Fort Peck again.

I got along fine. When I stopped to check my load I could hold on to the truck and go on around to check it. I felt kind of foolish when I got gas in Jordan, just sitting in the truck while the attendant filled my tank, and then his having to bring my change, too. I worried some that a patrolman might come along when I was checking my load. I'd sure get pulled over and be in trouble.

Velma figured things were worse than I had let on, and called Johnie, Rosalie's husband, to go and meet me when he got off work. But I was home by then. I had to crawl in the back door, but I made it. Of course, they took me to the hospital where I spent three days, then came home in a cast that I wore for three months.

Well, what to do? Can't just lay around when there's work to do. I took the office chair, put my knee on it, and wheeled myself around the store. I could cut meat. Only I could not carry anything heavy. But I could do most things in the store.

One time we went to the movie in Glasgow. As we came out of the theater I was holding on to the car to come down off the sidewalk, as I was having to use crutches. A girl who was parked right next to our car had backed up and was coming forward again. She hit our car and knocked me down. I wasn't hurt, but it caused quite a confusion for a couple of minutes.

While we were living in Fort Peck, Walt Vanderpan called and said Henry was in a coma and they couldn't find a doctor; and the hospital would not admit him without a doctor's order. The hospital suggested taking him to Plentywood, which is forty-three miles from Scobey. This did not make sense as we had two doctors in town. Doctor Norman was on vacation and Dr. Merle Fitz couldn't be found. I told Walt to wait and we would close up and come. We closed the store and drove to Scobey. It was a bad, cold night with rain and a strong wind. Someone said they thought Dr. Fitz had gone to Regina. We did not think he would take his plane in that kind of weather, but we went out to the airport. His plane was there. We called the port of entry north of Plentywood. They said no one fitting his description had gone through there. It was ten o'clock in the evening by this time, and that would have been the only customs office open at that hour. We didn't know what to do. Then someone who was watching his house saw a light in the window. He had been to Regina and come back through the port. He came down and gave Henry some gluten. Lydia had given Hank too much insulin. Henry had diabetes. While he was up and around, he controlled it. But he'd had a stroke and was in bed. We'd had him in the nursing home, but Lydia talked him into coming back to the shack. This was wrong but there was nothing we could do. He was looking at the money. He was generous with his money and helped a lot of people, but not himself. He would not have the doctor come to check him unless it was serious because he charged five dollars. The doctor charged Hank $60 for the gluten. Hank said, "Well, he got his alley paid for."

I owned a building next to Dr. Fitz. I was out on the farm when the city was doing some paving. Fitz and the others on the alley decided to have the alley paved. The pavers didn't pay any attention to what they were doing; and the way they left it, all the water would run into my basement. I had to get cement and build a wall to divert the water. I told Fitz I would never pay for my share of the paving because of that, and I never did. That's what Henry meant when he said Fitz had gotten his money for the alley.

As I mentioned before, Henry had had a stroke in the early 1960's. It was harvest time and he thought the barley was ready. I had been told that when you thought the barley was ready you should go fishing for two weeks, and then come home and cut it. When I got to the pickup to go to the farm, he was sitting in it pounding his knee with his hand. When we got to the farm, he had trouble walking. I wanted to take him back to town. He would not go. He thought we had to get that combine ready, which we did. Velma and the girls came out during the day. Karen cried when she saw Henry stumbling around, but he would not go into town with them. He thought we had to get in the field. Running the combine was his job, but he could not get up into it. I had to take it out. By the time I got the combine out to the field he was there with the truck. How he got into that old cab-over truck I'll never know, but he did. The barley was not ready. That left me to harvest it by myself. Henry would lay in bed and talk about what he would do when he got his strength back. I did not have the heart to tell him he would never get it back laying there. He lost when he left the home. They had him up walking.

1970's

We decided to sell the store as I was getting to Social Security age. This went on for about three months. We had one man looking at it for his son. They spent three days looking things over. The man figured the bank would give them the money. The bank wanted him to co-sign on the note, which he did not want to do. I couldn't figure that one out. Another man had a business he needed to sell first.

We sold to some local folks. He worked for the Corp of Engineers. The deal was no money down and $250 a month. The whole deal didn't make sense to me. I thought they'd want to pay more. They had gotten our old contract with the Corps of $25 a month rent; but remembering the 30's and the hard times, he was afraid. From my point of view and with what experience I had, I did not figure the paper was any good; but they were honest, and never missed a payment. I spent the money on the farm some way every month. That was kind of foolish when I think of it now, but there was machinery to buy.

We moved back to Henry's farm again in the fall of 1970. Paul Chabot had the deeded land rented at that time as he had bought the lease, which was still good for seven years, from Dexter. All we had was the thee hundred twenty acres of state land. Hank died that fall and left the land to me.

After Paul's lease ran out I rented the deeded land to Johnie. I still had the state land to farm. We moved a couple of bins I had bought onto the farm.

We put up a slant wall building, 40x80 feet. Johnie called me and said he could get this building from the Glasgow Air Force Base for fifty dollars. It had to be moved at once and we would have to remove the foundation which was thirty inches high and ten inches thick. I went down to see how hard it would be to break the concrete. It didn't seem too bad as the concrete has a lot of cracks in it. I told him to go ahead and buy it; but then someone decided it had not been properly advertised. They advertised and one bidder wanted them to pay $400 to take it out and another wanted $250. They asked Johnie what he'd give for it. He said he'd give $25. When he went in later, they told him to give them the $25. They had the papers all ready for him. The walls of the building were sixteen feet high. There were three sixteen foot wide overhead doors, two sixteen foot sliding doors, and a lot of windows. It was seventy-five miles from the farm. It was early winter and the days were short. Johnie helped me the first day; after that I was pretty much on my own. Most of the sheets were sixteen feet long and sixteen inches wide. It was an easy building to take down and put up. If those who had been interested had looked it over we would not have gotten it so cheap.

I was busy one morning at the start of taking it down. I was working on the roof caps. It was raining a little and I was getting wet, and decided I'd better get down. I discovered that I was on a roof covered with ice. It was a half mile to the base buildings and no one around. I didn't know what to do. I had a burlap sack I had been using to keep my knees a little dry. I took that and rubbed the ice off the roof till I was able to get down to my ladder. I was lucky the ice wasn't any thicker than it was.

106

I hauled a lot of the building home on the pickup. Johnie hauled some of the longer pieces to Glasgow to a friend's yard. When I got the roof and the walls down, the Corps of Engineers was satisfied as the building wasn't blocking the view of the planes coming in. I quit for the winter. In the spring, Johnie and some friends got the frame down using the Corps' machine. I took a truck and hauled the frame and long pieces home. The Corps took their tractor and pushed the concrete in to a low spot, no charge; and everybody was happy. The Corps was good to me at the base as it had been in Fort Peck. I spent the summer putting the building up. I had to make the foundation thirty inches high to have it high enough for the doors. I had a man come in with a crane to set up the frame. He only charged $120. Johnie helped him. About this time we decided to cement part of the floor. We got a load of cement; and when we had enough for the floor, we had part of a yard left. The driver said he'd just dump it in the doorway and we could wheel it to where we wanted it, as we had some places we needed to fill. That seemed like a good idea. We went into the house and paid him. When we came out and Johnie went in the building he said, "We've got to get busy and finish the floor." I said, "We've got to get this out the door!" They had brought a load of quick setting cement and did not tell us. They get this type of cement in the fall when the weather is freezing and must have had some left over. We got it out the door but the floor sure was a mess. But we were getting it looking more like a farm. Johnie got discouraged and decided to leave the farm and go back to Glasgow.

Then I rented the deeded land to another man, ten dollars an acre for all the land. Some were getting more, but I figured year in and year out it was all the land was worth, or all it would pay. He made the payment due on October 1. I told him that was too early as sometimes you still have harvesting to do, or at least work to be done. But he said that's the way he wanted it. He did a poor job of farming; mostly he was after government payments. Then the price of wheat went up and it looked to me like we might be in for inflation. I asked him to take a sliding price based on what it was when he leased it. He would not consider it so I cancelled his lease. He had forgotten about the October first date on his contract and had forgotten to pay me on time. He got three or four years on his ten-year lease.

Then I rented the land out to another man on crop share, and have a good renter. He farms good and keeps the land as clean of weeds as possible.

Meanwhile, I continued to farm the state land through hail, grasshoppers, and drought. One year I finished seeding and the wheat was just coming up real nice when we went to the West Coast to see the family. When we got home everything was plumb black, not a spear of wheat. The hoppers had taken everything. That was the biggest crop I ever raised, and no harvest expenses. The crop insurance and government payments were more than I could have gotten out of an average crop.

The basement of our house on the farm is not a full basement. I had one wall that was not finished. I thought I could run a shoot through the window to pour cement down. It did not work. We had to carry it over in five-gallon buckets. The truck driver helped us and it did not turn out too bad. This was quick setting cement also.

I had Jim Gebhardt and Homer Powell dig us a well at this time. Jim liked a steel casing. I got one for him and started to make holes for the water to come in. They told me to go home. They had plenty of time to do that. I could never get more than two hundred gallons of water at a time. I have often wondered if they punched the holes the wrong way. If they punched them down, the pea gravel would fall into the holes and plug them up. The next year Jim was digging a well for Quentin McCarty. This time he used plastic pipe. Quentin and I spent a day of driving trying to find the right size pipe. In our time of driving he tried to talk me into having another well dug. I wasn't too anxious to do that as I would have to dig it away from the house and run a pipe to the house. So I just kind of let things slide. One day I met Quentin in Scobey. He said, "When are we going to dig that well?" He looked up and there was Jim. Jim said the drilling rig was at one of the neighbor's and they were through with it; and for me to go and get it, and he'd come when he had the time. But Quentin said, "Let's go ahead and start." I borrowed a tractor from a neighbor to turn the machine, and we went to work. We got down about three feet and hit a big rock. We moved over a few feet and it went pretty good. Quentin ran the machine and I hauled the dirt. We got down about thirty feet and the pipes that go down in the well to turn the machine broke. We were just using one strand of number nine wire, but this was an old machine and the pipes were brittle. We went over to see Jim. He told us to take the hooks and what was needed; and he'd come over and help us fish it out, which he did. He stayed then and ran the machine. We got down about eighty feet and the rods broke again. Everything went down this time and the bucket was stuck in the bottom of the well. Velma came out and said supper was ready. Jim said, "We can't eat now. If we don't get this out tonight, we won't ever get it out." He put all the strain he thought the cable would stand into turning the machine. Then he got a hydraulic jack and started to jack up the machine. Now we'll go eat. When we got up the next morning, Jim already had the bucket and most everything else out of the well.

Jim wanted a wood curbing on the well. I was fortunate enough to get some redwood, two-inch flooring. It had some knots in it and I got a good price on it. I had to get busy and bevel the corners and make the curbing. We got a good well this time, with lots of water. Jim never charged me for anything. He has plenty of money and enjoys a few days of home cooking.

I made a bid, to the estate, on an old house in Scobey. The bid was for $12,000. They refused the bid as it seems they had $18,000 on their minds. Too much for me. A year later they called me and said I could have it for $12,000. We bought it. If they had waited a few days they could have gotten $15,000, but they didn't know that.

We started to remodel. We planned to enlarge the house. We got a contractor to dig more basement. He wanted $5600. I told him I'd pay him $6000 to dig the basement and do the cement work. Then they were to help me move two walls and put in the support to hold up the ceiling and roof on the end where we were extending, as I did not know how to put this in without a wall, which would not be there. They agreed. This old house had stucco on the walls and I proceeded to take it off of some of them.

We were joining the roof and would have a valley there. I wanted to leave the shingles on the old part and slip the valley tin under them. My contractor said it couldn't be done. So I had to do it. Yes, it can be done. We, Velma doing most of the work, took all the lath and plaster off the inside walls.

To save winter driving, we moved into the hotel in town for a month and put in some long days on the house. I did my own wiring, and hired the local plumber to put in most of the plumbing.

One day when I was working on the roof, the contractor's wife came by and wanted $185. She said Bud, the man who had done the digging, had run into something that was more than he expected. I told her, "I know, and you know, I have no business to pay this as I had a contract for the job." She got so mad she walked away; and for a year or two, if I went into a building she'd go out.

Her husband came around to see me and I told him my complaints. They were to back-fill on the walls which had not been taken care of. I had a seam in my basement floor which should not have been there. They had hauled my dirt away, some of which I needed. He promised to take care of my complaints and I paid him the $185, but he said the dirt belonged to the diggers. My other problems were not taken care of, and I had to finish them myself.

We insulated the walls and put on sheet rock. Then I put on another wall and finished it the same way. Double walls. As the plumber said, "A house inside of a house."

Johnie came and helped me put on the steel siding, and we got triple glass windows. We have a house that is cooler in the summer and warmer in the winter. We have no air conditioner.

After this, I added on to the old garage by the alley, put some steel siding on it, some windows, and shingled the roof. I had some men help pour the driveway.

I had a couple of local so-called carpenters pour the floor and driveway to the garage by the house. I came in from the farm one evening and one of them said, "We thought we'd just leave the curb as it is. You can put a 2x6 down there." There was a drop off to the street. I didn't say anything. When they left I took my sledge hammer and knocked the curb down. One of the men came back later and said, "I talked to a man about that and was going to do that." I said, "Well, it's done now." But when they finished it off they could just as well have left the curb, as the drop off is almost as bad. I never had too good of luck having work done by someone else.

Velma had always done the perfa-taping on the walls of all the houses we worked on; but at her age, it was too much for her in this house. I didn't want to get into the perfa-taping. I asked a lumber dealer if there was someone he thought would give me a good job. He told me of a man that was fast and good, so he thought. We made a deal for fourteen cents a foot. He did one bedroom which came somewhere in the sixty dollar range. He said, "That's not much money for that room." But that's what he had asked for. Then he didn't want to finish the job. He said the nails were not driven in deep enough. I told him I could take care of that, if that was a problem. Then the cracks were too wide and took too much filler. Of course, what he wanted was more money, so I gave him a couple cents more and got a terrible job. He didn't know too much about what he was doing.

We have a window about ten feet by five feet with triple glass. When the glass for it was delivered, it was broken, and another had to be ordered. The glass came from a window manufacturer in Williston. They called and said they had the glass and we made a date to pick up the window. I asked some neighbors and friends to come and help me put it in, as it was heavy. So we were all set to take it off the pickup. When we got to Williston, they had not started to put the window together, and we had these people coming to help unload it at 4 P.M. They got busy, and said they'd have it done by 1 P.M. which would give us time to get home. When they finally got us loaded, it was closer to 2 P.M. Johnie was doing the driving. I never expected the window to get home all in one piece, but it did; and we got there before everyone got disgusted and left. We got the window in.

Velma wanted a white house with a red roof. I could not get any red shingles. I had to paint the roof. I got some red paint and went to work. The new shingles didn't do too bad, but the old ones just wouldn't hold the paint. I put enough paint on those old shingles for two or three houses, but no good. Too much dirt from the 1930's. I finally had to change them all. I had three different sections of the roof each about one hundred square feet. I had the shingles. I called a local contractor. He said he would do the job for $630; but he had a building to put up, and wouldn't have time until fall. I asked another man who said he'd do it for the $630, but not until September as it was too hot. I told him he could work in the cool of the day, but he had an outdoor toilet to build at Fort Peck. I got my hammer and went to work. I had a tarp that would cover the area I was working on. I took the old shingles off, and put the new ones on, with some help from Johnie and my granddaughter, Michele. Got it painted right away, got a good job done, and saved $1000, figuring the painting. However, a storm came up and the rain caused some of the paint to run onto the white siding. Velma didn't like to have me on the roof.

In the mid-eighties I sold the lease on the state land. At that time, it was all I was farming. I had the rest rented out to a good renter who takes care of all the government bookwork. My buildings were all paid for. I had to keep a full line of machinery to farm the ground, and was paying taxes on the machinery. Also, Dr. Fitz said that Velma should not be living so far away from a doctor. This is why we decided to move to town.

Corinne   Karen   Rosalie   Melba
Melvin   Velma
1994

1990's
Germany

In the late eighties and until the Gulf War, Michele was living in Germany where her husband, Rick Riehl, was stationed in the army. They lived in a small farming community out of Osterholz-Scharmbeck, near Bremen. Dexter and Corinne wanted to go visit, and I wanted to go and see what I could find out about my family. In September of 1990, Andrea, Corinne, Dexter, Velma, and I flew out of Seattle on Northwest Airlines to Frankfurt. This worked well for us as Melba was living in Seattle and we could leave the car at their house and they could take us to the airport and pick us up when we came back. We had a layover in Boston, but never left the terminal. So we had no problems except that it was a long ride. We got to Frankfurt early in the day, so Michele took us to see the Heidelberg Castle. She tried to go up a narrow street about like an alley. It was so low because of the buildings hanging out over it. She got the roof of the van stuck, but managed to get it backed up with no visible damage. Michele had to park about a half mile from the castle. It seems there is no place to park cars near it. We had to hire a taxi. It took two trips to get us all there and it took a lot of marks to pay the driver. Dexter paid so I don't know how much it cost. Velma could not go through the castle as it was hard walking. Michele stayed with her. One thing I could not understand: they had big windows, no glass. What they used way back then I never found out. On the return trip in the taxi, Dexter lost his camera. It fell out of his pocket and was left in the taxi.

We went down to the town square and information center. There were hundreds of bicycles parked there. It seemed everybody rode a bike. I never did find out how they knew which one was theirs. There were four hotels there; only one had any rooms left. It cost me three hundred marks for the two rooms and five marks to park off the street. For breakfast, we had a hard roll, boiled egg, sausage, jam and a short cup of coffee. On the way to north Germany we stopped at a place where they had a long counter where you picked up what you wanted, cafeteria style. There was a coffee machine at the end of the counter. Velma was first. She pushed the button on the machine and got her part cup of coffee. I thought I'd give mine an extra shot and fill it up. This started the machine all over again. The woman behind the counter started hollering, "Nein! Nein!" Without thinking, I gave the button another push to stop the coffee. This just sent another cup of coffee out of the machine, running everywhere. The woman started again, "Gay! Gay!" I got out of there. Dexter was paying so I don't know what it cost. Velma and I were planning to rent a room, as Michele only had room for three people. But she had an attic, and Corinne and Dexter slept up there.

Siggelkow, Mecklenburg, Germany

Dexter, Corinne and I took a two day trip into East Germany. The wall had been down for about a year. We found the town of Siggelkow which was founded in 1250. We found the graveyard, but there were no Siggelkows buried there. Corinne noticed that there were no old graves, the oldest dating back to the 1940's. We found a town office where a man and woman worked. I have a letter from the port at Hamburg with the passenger list. This helped us a lot. I'd show them the letter and they could see what we wanted. The lady said, "A last I see a real Siggelkow." We couldn't learn anything from them. They gave us a telephone number of a couple from Rochester, Minnesota who were also searching for information.

We went on to Stavenhagen where my dad was supposed to have come from, a town of about ten thousand people, and a town square where you could park. The streets and the town center all were made of field stones and were hard to walk on. They had two hotels. Both said, "nein." We went back a few miles on the road we had taken into town. We saw a sign, "Hostel." Dexter drove over to it. It was a big building with three wings. I think it had been an agricultural college. Corinne and I took the first wing. It had a lot of young folk around. We tried the next one. The door was locked. We asked someone where the hostel was. They told us to go to the next door. It was open but no one was around. Corinne found a woman who took us to two rooms and said, "Breakfast at eight." The bedding was at the bottom of the bed and you made your own bed. There was a wash basin in the room. For anything else, you had to go to the public facilities. We had a better breakfast than what we had gotten in West Germany. Now we had to find someone to pay. Corinne found the lady, and she took us back to a man at a desk. He said, "Keys." The rooms were pretty cheap, around twenty dollars or less.

Now, back to Stavenhagen and what we came for. We found the church. The door was locked and the building was in disrepair. The minister wasn't around. We found the town office. No one spoke English. They sent over to a school for a lady who was an English teacher. She did not appear to be too friendly. She asked us if we were there to claim property that had once been in our family. It seems that there have been a lot of people coming there hoping to find something they could lay claim to. She was so happy when we told her we were not looking for an estate, just information. She became quite friendly, and she and Corinne had a nice visit after that; but there was no way they could help us find out anything about the Siggelkows. They told us they had no records there. All the records were in the next town, Malchin. They sent a girl with us to go back to the church. We found the minister at home and visited with him. But it's true. There are no records and no graves. He said they don't have the room in Germany that we have in our country, so the graveyards are reused.

We went on to Malchin. We went to the town hall. This time they sent out for a school administrator who could speak English. They took us down to the basement where records were kept, but there was nothing before 1900. He told us to go back to Stavenhagen and try some more, and if not successful to come and he would try some more. We spent two days looking for graves that weren't there. We returned to West Germany, not much wiser. There are a lot of Siggelkows in a church directory at Schwerin, dating back to the sixteenth century; but that's over a hundred miles from where my folks lived.

We went to see an old church in Bremen. We had to walk about a quarter or half a mile to get to the church from where we could park. This church was a round building. It was started in the eleventh century. It's called Unser Lieben Frauen. We had to follow the church around until we found a door that was not locked. There was a lady there at a desk. She told us the history of the church as well as some of her personal history. She was a very staunch Protestant. She had two sons, one married to a Roman Catholic and the other to a Latter Day Saint. Corinne and Dexter wanted to see some of the other buildings in the area. The walking is hard on those cobblestones, and Velma had about enough walking. As they walked faster than we did, they told us to start out and they would meet us at the car. Coming out of the round church, with streets coming in from all directions, I had no way to know how far we had come. I had no idea which street to take. With Velma to watch out for, I just had to stay put. I stayed outside to try and catch Corinne and Dexter as they came by. Boy, was it cold, that wind coming in from the North Sea. Velma complained about having to sit in the cathedral and listen to that woman, but I would have gladly changed places with her. Dexter and Corinne came by and we got back to the car.

Churches seem to be my bad luck. One day, the five of us (Michele stayed home.) went to find Martin Luther's church south of Berlin at Wittenberg. We saw a big church and Dexter found a parking spot a couple blocks from it. We left Velma in the car and walked over to the church and discovered that there was parking at the church. Dexter said, "Why don't you bring the car here?" and gave me the keys. It made sense. The car we were using was a new VW. It was parked about fifteen feet back from a steep bank. I started it and tried to find reverse. I failed every time, and each time I got a little closer to the bank. A man standing there backed it out for me but faced it the wrong way. I did not want to go towards town. I went across the street through the intersection where there were some old sheds that did not seem to be in use. I pulled up to them forgetting I still did not know how to find reverse. All I could do was leave it. Dexter and Corinne came by. It had been the wrong church. It was not the church where Luther had his pastorship, but was the Castle Church, where he had nailed his ninety-five thesis. Dexter parked the car and we walked up to the town square about two blocks. Dexter and Corinne went on to find the church. The square was a busy place. Those people hadn't been able to get anything for years, and there were vans from all over with things to sell. I found a bench out of the wind, but pretty soon Velma got to worrying that the others would be waiting at the car. I hung on as long as I could. I finally gave in and down to the car we went. Of course, it was locked and no place to sit down. There was a kind of stand there where they sold beer. There was a table with some chairs. Some men were sitting and drinking beer. I told Velma when they left we would sit down. We did, but it was cold in that wind.

On the way back to Michele's we had to follow a bunch of Russian army trucks for some miles. There were still about thirty thousand troops in that area of Germany. It was a long day by the time we got home.

We went to the North Sea one Sunday afternoon. Nothing much there but miles of grass with a few cows on it, some windmills for generating electricity, and a cold north wind.

Michele thought we should go out and have a real German meal. Velma and I just had some regular food. The others had the German meal. I got finished eating before the rest did, and went out to the cash register to talk to the innkeeper. He could speak pretty good English. I kind of wanted to talk to the old man, but his wife brought me the bill and I paid it. It was one hundred ten marks which would be about sixty-eight dollars. Then the rest of the party came out and it was time to go. This place was in a little town about a mile from where Michele lived. Velma and I walked up there a couple of times. There was a path through the woods. I went up a couple of times thinking I might get to talk to the man at the inn, but he was never around. I was told if I was going to be in there I had to buy coffee or something. A young man came in to use the phone, and lit a cigarette. The next thing I heard the woman say was, "Well, I don't like it!" Then she told him he'd have to buy something. He left. I asked her if there was any place where a person could buy a hamburger. She said there was and tried to tell me where. I spent a couple of hours looking, but could never find a place that was open that sold hamburgers. I stopped a few times at the bar hoping to see the old man, but he was never there, and his wife was not too friendly.

We went to the army base a few times. We could not get into the commissary to buy anything unless Michele or someone with a pass was with us. There was a car rental, novelty store, and a Dodge car sales there. The car salesman, an Irishman right from Ireland, was a good friend of Michele's. As soon as we came in he would go out and get some rolls. I told him one day I should not be eating his rolls, as I drove a Toyota. He said, "Give me back my rolls!" We had a birthday party for Dexter, myself and Tyler. He was the only one there who was not family.

The small country roads were just one lane. When two cars meet, someone has to turn out. The yellow reflectors tell you who has the right of way.

When we left Michele's to go back to the States, we used a car as it was a lot cheaper than the van we had come in. We were over loaded as there were six of us in the car. Andrea kind of got down out of sight as much as she could. We made it to the airport. We were lucky on our flight back as there were some storms going over to Germany and we had to go out of our way. But we finally got to Boston. I guess Boston has only one wheelchair. They asked me if I could get Velma to a certain point. When I'd get there, no wheelchair. This went on until we got to customs. Then the fun began. Dexter and Corinne went to clear us through. They came back and said they needed our papers, and left us again. We were stuck. We could not go back or ahead. We waited and waited. Finally Velma said she was thirsty. I went to the desk. They didn't know where I could get any water. I started to walk around and saw a fountain, but no way to get the water to Velma. A lady came and said, "What are you doing here?" I told her I was looking for some water for my wife. She did not know of any, but she was only thirty feet from the fountain. I got worried about how much time we had left. I went over to information. I knew our flight number, but they said I would have to go upstairs to Northwest to find out the information I wanted. So we just waited. They finally came with a wheelchair, a man to push it, and the works. We got through customs but my coat or something got left behind. I went back to get it. I had to go through the whole thing again: watch and everything in a bowl. When I came back through, I reached for a bowl I thought was mine, but it was not. Got that straightened out and got on the plane for Seattle.

The Last Years

In the spring, 1991, Velma and I went to the West Coast for a visit. Corinne, Dexter, and Dexter's brother's family wanted to have a picnic up in the Blue Mountains at Cutsforth Park, so we went with them. They pulled a small camper up there and were going to have a good time. It was so cold, Velma and Dexter's mother sat in the camper with a Coleman heater trying to keep their feet warm. The rest of the folks kept warm through activity. I just wandered around watching the kids, trying to keep warm. There was a fast little stream in the canyon. Some of these kids were pretty small and no one seemed to be watching them. They were about halfway down the bank to the stream. One little boy about four years old was full of the dickens and I thought if I told them to come up he might just head down. I thought I'd get below him. I stepped out on those pine needles and the next thing I knew I was on the bottom of that canyon with my head in a pile of sand. My thoughts were that I was going to suffocate, but I came to enough to get out. Michele came down to help me. Then Dexter came and they got me up the bank. It was about time to go. We went to Dexter's home. After a while I did not feel too bad. I drove to Seattle the next day, and then I drove back to Scobey. The bolts had gotten loose on the opener of the door to the old garage. When I put it together it was out of line and stayed down about a foot. I had not gotten around to adjusting it. I was working in and out of the garage and bumped my head twice on that door. Then I was in trouble. I went to Doctor Thomas. He looked at me and said, "There's nothing wrong with you, and if there was, an x-ray would not show it." I went to Glasgow. They took an x-ray, and three people looked at it and saw nothing wrong. A week later they called me and said to come down and see the doctor. They said I had one vertebra out. They had me lift a little and gave me a light massage. They told me to call in about five days and tell them how I felt. I called a massager I know and asked him if he thought he could help me. He said he thought he could. This was Mr. Prewett in Glasgow. I went to see him. He worked on me for about fifteen minutes and then used the vibratory. He said he was not going to try and put any vertebrae back that day. He put one in and it did not stay. He did not say anything about another appointment. I waited a couple of days, called and got another appointment. This time he put two in and they stayed. We were leaving for North Carolina to see Karen and her family and I did not get to go back to him. I still had one more out of place. It bothered me for a long time, but it has about quit now. The hospital was going to put a collar on me. I am sure this would have cost medicare over a thousand dollars before they got through. Mr. Prewett charged me fifty dollars.

We were down to North Carolina to visit Karen. Her insurance company had bought her a home gym machine. I used it a few times and decided to get one. We went to Sears. They had one on sale for two hundred fifty dollars. Karen thought it was all right. I bought it, but when we went in the back room to get it they did not have any in stock, and of course, they would not let me have the one on the floor. But they would have one down from Greensboro the next day. We went down to pick it up. No machine, but they would have one from another town in three or four days. When we went to get it, no machine. The salesman said he could not tell us when they would have it, but when it came in they would ship it to me and pay the freight charges. I told him I did not think UPS would take it. He said they would. Well, they should know. I asked them to give me my money back. No, they could not do that. Back home, I waited a couple of weeks and called. They had been trying to get me on the phone, they said, and would get it right out. I waited a couple more weeks and had Karen call them. They told her UPS would not take it as it was too heavy. They would have to ship it by freight and it would have to go through California. I hauled freight for the railroad for sixteen years and never heard of that route. They should know. A couple more weeks, and they had lost it and had to send a tracer after it. Then they said they could not find it and would have to give me my money back. I called Karen and told her to pick the machine up and I would get it some time when we were down there. She got it and put it in two boxes and shipped it to me UPS. Too much for Sears to do. It cost me thirty-eight dollars and Sears nothing. I told Karen to tell them I wanted twenty dollars for phone calls. They just laughed at her. The machine I got from Sears was a belt type and the maintenance was too expensive even for the little I used it. I bought another machine, but not from Sears. I used to buy from Sears, but no more. I bought the next one in Carolina too. I bought it on sale with a senior citizen discount. Including sales tax, it cost me two hundred thirty-eight dollars. It has weights and cables. I brought it home. I won't tell here what I had to do, but I rebuilt that machine and it works good. I did not mind the extra work as I got a four hundred dollar machine.

On the first day of January, 1994, I put Velma in the nursing home. I went in with her as that was the easiest way to get her to go. That was only fourteen dollars more. I slept there and ate some meals with her. We stayed there until the weather warmed up in the spring. Then we moved back to our house. Rosalie came in June to help me with her.

Velma was not happy here at home. She had always been right in there doing more than her share. Now all she could do was sit in a chair while we went about doing things, and she felt she was not one of the family. Melba and Rosalie were helping me then. We took her down town twice a day. We had no problem with her health. We kept her weight the same and she had no blood pressure problems. Velma felt no one loved her any more. Most of the time she just called Melba and Rosalie "that girl." As for myself, the last three years I got two to four hours of sleep a day. She always wanted me near her, and if I dozed off, she would say, "Are you sleeping?" I suppose I was indifferent at times. I was so tired and guess I thought she should understand. She just needed too much for me to give. Sometimes I got a little cross with her. But I realized it wasn't her fault, and by the time she passed away I went along with her as far as I could. But I had not enough to give. I could not take care of her as she could not move herself to help me. She lost that portion of her mind. Alzheimer's is a terrible disease.

Louis's wife, Amanda, had the same problem. One time as they were driving down to see us, all day long she told him he was going the wrong way and they'd soon run into the Pacific Ocean. We stopped at their home one time and she kept pestering him to go to the store for something for us hungry people. He kept telling her the freezer was full, and there was no need for the store. We stopped to see Amanda one time after Louis died. She saw me and all she would say was, "Daddy." She thought I was Louis. Dorothy Swanson, who was also there, could do nothing to distract her attention. I guess there was a resemblance between Louis and I. I never could see it, but we stopped in Missouri one time at their daughter Ruth's, and she said to me that when I came in it was just like her dad walking through the door.

We kept Mom home for ten months more without insurance before we put her in the last time in the fall of 1995. Melba was moving and Rosalie had to have an operation on her foot. I had planned to take her down town, just as we had done before. There were benches every two blocks where she could stop and rest if she got tired. I took her down, but when we got back to the home she wanted to go home with me. I told her I couldn't take her. She said, "You mean I can't go." I said, "No. I have no one to help me and I can't take care of you by myself." As I headed for the door she was right ahead of me. I turned and went back through another door and left her standing there, maybe one of the hardest things I've ever had to do in my life.

Some time later when Corinne and Andrea were visiting, we all went down for a coffee break. On the way back up to the nursing home we had a good time singing; but when we made a move to go Velma was right with us. Finally Corinne said, "Why don't I stay here and visit, and you go home." We did, and when Velma got her supper, Corinne left. Many times Velma would ask me if I'd brought the car, or would she have to get her shoes on so she could walk. After sixty years of sharing, it's hard to say no.

I would go up about five-thirty each day. After she got through eating, I would sit with her until she wanted to go to her room. I'd take her down to the room and put her to bed and sing to her until she went to sleep. Most of the nurses were very considerate. They would watch, and while I was getting her in bed, they would bring her sleeping pill. That way I could go home around nine. Once in a while they would come about ten, making it pretty late.

The night she died I went to help Velma with her supper. She ate most of it. As before, I had been singing to her. I sang a couple of short songs before she had her stroke. She used to sing along with me. I thought that now that she was not able to sing it might make her feel bad, so I stopped. Her eyesight must have been about gone. She was feeling on the table like she wanted something. I asked her if she wanted a drink of water. She nodded. I gave her a couple of drinks. She sat back in her chair and seemed to want to go to sleep; then gave a gasp, threw her head over the side of the chair. Three more choking gasps. I called the nurse. By the time she got her checked she said, "She's gone." I walked to the house and told Melba. Ann Roberts took Melba up to see her before they took her to the morgue. Then Melba got busy. It was Thursday night, May 30, 1996. The funeral was on Monday. We had to get all our business done on Friday. I don't know what I would have done if Melba had not been here.

Later in the summer of 1996, after Velma died, Johnie and Rosalie Holding were taking a motor home to Texas to his sister, and they took me along. We ran out of gas twenty miles this side of Miles City. John had filled both tanks the night before and should have still had fuel. The tanks sounded empty. We were lucky there was a big ranch there where we ran out, and they sold us some gas. When we went to fill up the second tank, it was still full. We drove to Texas on one tank, as the fuel would not draw from the other one. We got along fine until we got to Denver. We were not getting enough gas. It took us three hours to get to the next town, sixty miles from Denver. John got that fixed. Another couple hours lost. We stopped in Amarillo with some of John's and Rosalie's friends. We got the air conditioner fixed, which helped some. John couldn't get a two-wheel trailer in Glasgow, and he had to take a full trailer which pulled harder and cost more. They told him if he saw a smaller one while he was on the road, he could switch and get a refund. He saw one and stopped. This was five in the afternoon. The place was closed, but we called and they said they would be there at six. They got there at seven. John got busy making the change, and the lady got busy with the paper work. Something did not look right to me. I went out and told John to wait a while. When she got through she wanted sixty dollars more than he had already paid. We only had three or four hundred miles to go, so decided against the trade. Another three hours lost. John was having trouble. It would go into overdrive and stay there until it got ready to come out. I suggested we have it disconnected. He pulled into a Chevy garage. The mechanic told John he had no problem. There was a fan in there that came on when the motor got to a certain temperature, and made a noise like that. Pulling that car on that trailer in that heat was a little too much. We stayed a couple days in Texas, then went home in two days. It was a rough trip for me. My blood pressure went way up, and the further we got the worse it got. But I saw a lot of dry country.

After a while I decided to go to the West Coast to visit Corinne's, Melba's and Audrey's families. I went down to the station where I have a card to get gas. I could not get my card to work. I went to Conoco. They had just had some new pumps installed. They had a sign: For information on pumps see attendant inside. I figured I'd forget half of what he'd tell me by the time I got back to the pumps. I went home to bed. I had half a tank of gas, enough to get me to Glasgow, but I wanted to take a short cut. I did not leave as early as I normally do so I could get gas at one of the towns west of Scobey. I got to Malta about eleven and visited Velma's niece, Ruth Flansaas. Then her husband, John, came home and we had lunch. I left there about one. As it was getting late, I thought I would stop in Great Falls, but I drove too fast and got there around four, too early to stop. I went on to Missoula. I was tired, as I had slept very little the night before. While Velma was alive I was getting from two to four hours of sleep a day. The situation aggravated me so much I could not sleep. I would go to bed, sleep one hour then lay there until morning and time to get up. It took me a year after she died to start getting back to some sleep. Well, my windshield had a lot of bugs on it, but I thought I'd be stopping soon anyway. I did not stop to clean it. I got to Missoula, took a wrong turn, and got on the freeway going out. I had to go out a ways to get turned around. I got back to Missoula and turned off the freeway onto Reserve Street. I was told that if I crossed over the overpass and turned left to the next street, there was a cheaper motel there. I found no motel there. I drove out a ways, turned around, and came back. I forgot I had left Reserve Street and could not get on the freeway from that street. I drove out a ways, got turned again, stopped at a Super Eight, and asked the man how much it cost for one person to sleep. He said it cost forty-four dollars and twenty cents. I could have gotten a room for a little less in Missoula, but I decided to go on to a smaller town. Back to Reserve Street and the freeway. Still a dirty windshield. I intended to stop in Alberton but again I turned too soon and headed back to Missoula, got turned around and went on to Superior. I stopped at a motel there, but it was full. I was told there were two motels six blocks over in the old part of town. There was a big old hotel building with a motel sign on it. I pulled up to the door, went in, and asked the lady how much it would cost for me to sleep. She said, "Are you alone?" I said I was. She said, "No one with you?" I said no. She said the room would cost eighteen dollars plus tax. This was for a room in the old hotel part. This lady has several motel units besides the hotel, and has a couple of rooms in the hotel made into double units with bathrooms in them. (I think we've stayed in all of them now when I've traveled with one of the girls. They were all nice. She charged less than thirty dollars for both of us.) I was so tired, having driven over six hundred miles, that when I came out of my room to go to the bathroom, it seemed the exit was on the wrong end of the hall. In the morning, I came out the exit thinking I had to go around the building to get to my car. I came out the door, paying no attention to the cars that were parked there. I walked all around the building and there was my car. Then I realized I had forgotten my bag. I was still not thinking. Once more I went around the building back to the main door, which was the one I had come out of in the first place. I got my bag and was on my way. This was three or four months after Velma died. Over the years people have told me I had to get away for a while. A doctor whose mother had Alzheimer's said, "You have to get away for a month or two." A lady used to stop when we met on the street and tell me, "You have to give up. You can't help her and you are sacrificing your life for something you can't change." At the time I did not know this lady had lost both her parents. Her mother had Alzheimer's. Her dad kept his wife home. By the time he put her into the nursing home he stayed there, too. Just sat there in a chair. After she died, he died a couple of weeks later. He had put too much out. From what I have just written,

Melvin with his great-grandson, Remy Bernier-Lucien. December 25. 1998

one can see how far I had gone without realizing it.

After coming back from the West, I wanted to go down to see Karen before winter set in. Greg, Melba's youngest son went with me. We had no trouble going down. Ed was out of a job at that time. Greg went with him when he went to sign up for employment, and he got a job. He decided to stay in North Carolina to work. Johnie and Rosalie drove Greg's pickup down for him and rode back to Montana with me. Rosalie got to see Karen.

Melvin had a heart attack on August 7, 1998, from which he never fully recovered. Rosalie took him to Oregon to visit Corinne and Audrey in October. He spent his last Christmas with Karen in Memphis, Tennessee. He died February 9, 1999.

He is missed.

Appendix 1
Maps

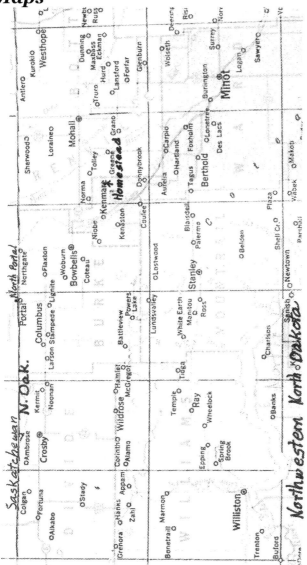

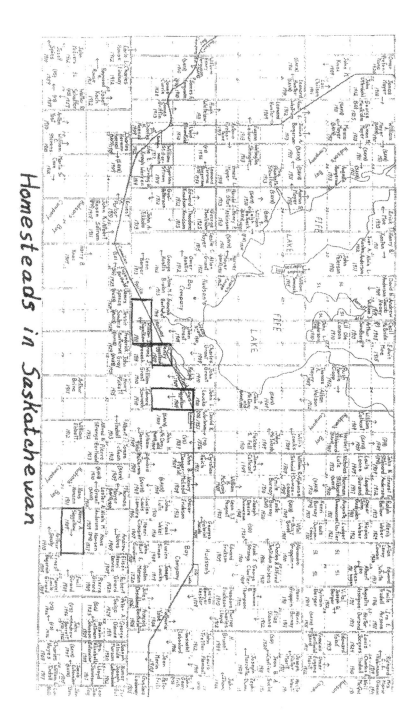

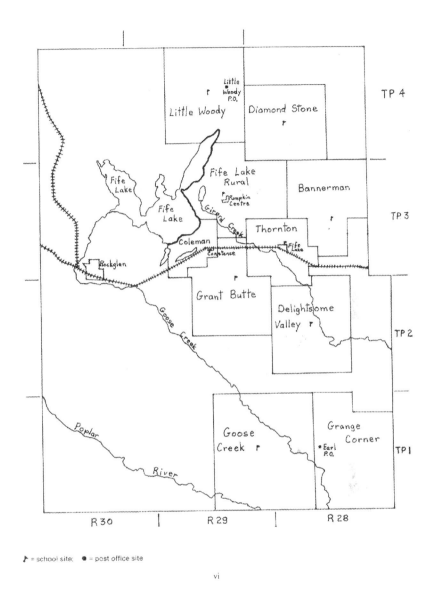

Little
Woody
P.O.

Little Woody

Diamond Stone

TP 4

Fife Lake
Rural

Fife
Lake

Pumpkin
Centre

Bannerman

TP 3

Fife
Lake

Girard Creek

Thornton

Fife
Lake

Coleman

Constance

Rockglen

Grant Butte

Delightsome
Valley

TP 2

Goose Creek

Poplar

River

Goose
Creek

Grange
Corner

Earl
P.O.

TP 1

R 30   R 29   R 28

♪ = school site;   ● = post office site

My first school - Delightsome Valley

My second school – Fife Lake

We lived on the eastern boundary of Grant Butte School District.

TRAILS USED BY EARLY PIONEERS

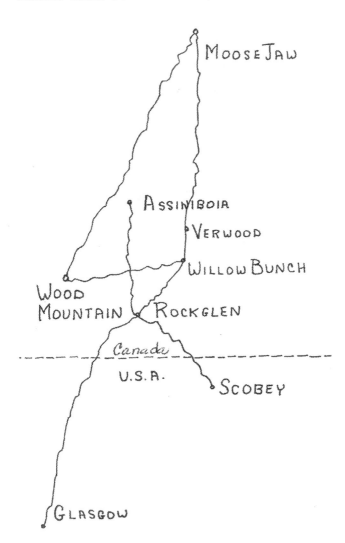

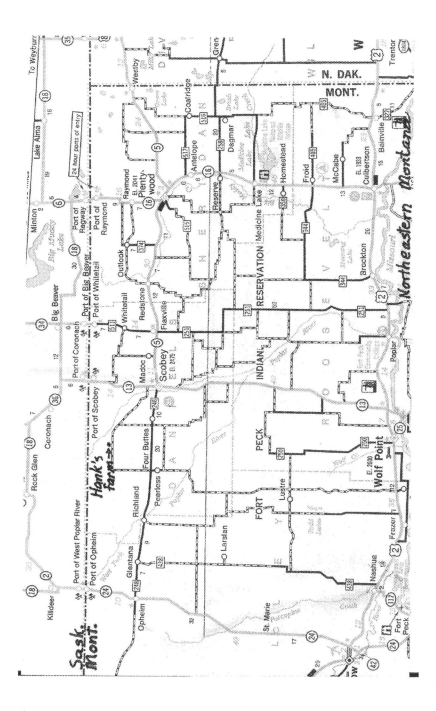

Northeastern Montana

Appendix 2
Melvin's Descendants

Melvin Emil Siggelkow = Velma Belle Draper
b. 20 Sept 1904   b. 10 June 1911
         m. 31 Oct 1936
d. 9 Feb 1999   d. 30 May 1996

Children of Melvin and Velma:
Rosalie Louise = Johnie Paul Holding
b. 30 Sept 1937   b. 24 Aug 1930
      m. 9 July 1960
           d. 10 Apr 2008

Corinne Mavis = Dexter Martin Miles
b. 18 May 1940   b. 22 Sept 1939
      m. 30 Dec 1962

Melba Joanne = Clair Eugene Folckomer
b. 18 Nov 1943   b. 2 May 1939
      m. 10 June 1962

Karen Jane = Edward Bernier
b. 15 Oct 1946   b. 9 Apr 1942
      m. 16 Aug 1967

Child of Rosalie Siggelkow and Johnie Holding:
Lisa Sue
b. 26 Aug 1972

Children of Corinne Siggelkow and Dexter Miles
Darrell Lee Miles = Trina Lynn Hellberg
b. 5 Oct 1963   b. 10 Apr 1969
      m. 6 June 1998
           Children of Darrell Miles and Trina Hellberg:
           Daniel Otto b.14 Jan 2001
           Andrew Max b. 5 Dec 2002
           Hans Ethan b. 20 Nov 2004
           Kyia Corinne b. 24 Feb 2007
           Soren Lee b. 6 Oct 2008

Craig Allen = Tawny Lynn Wilson
b. 1 Dec 1964   b. 18 Mar 1965
          m. 19 May 1985
                    Children of Craig Miles and Tawny Wilson:
                    Amanda Dawn b. 6 July 1988
                    Trent Allen b. 8 Mar 1990
                    Shane Matthew b. 30 June 1995

Carla Annette = Roger Perry Morter
b. 16 Feb 1966   b. 28 July 1965
          m. 7 Sept 1985
                    Children of Carla Miles and Roger Morter
                    Julie Ann b. 30 May 1986
                    Brian Lee b. 24 Sept 1987
                    Chelsie Marie b. 10 Dec 1989
                    Kailey Lyn b. 16 July 1992
                    Preston Thomas b. 4 July 1994
                    Carson Matthew b. 16 Oct 1996

Michele Noel = Richard Alexander Riehl
b. 24 Dec 1967   b. 18 May 1967
          m. 15 Aug 1987
d. 27 Feb 2009
                    Children of Michele Miles and Richard Riehl
                    Tyler Alexander b. 22 Sept 1989
                    Theresa Korine b. 4 Aug 1994

Andrea Joy = Carmelo Anthony Di Salvo
b. 23 Oct 1977   b. 7 March 1967
          m. 29 June 2002
                    Child of Andrea Miles and Carmelo Di Salvo
                    Moira Stefana b. 16 May 2008

Children of Melba Siggelkow and Clair Folckomer
Nadine Rae
b. 1 Aug 1964
          m. (1) Mark White; 9 Nov 1984
                    Child of Nadine Folckomer and Mark White:
                    Stephan Andrew White b. 30 July 1985
          (2) John Haskett 28 May

b. 28 Sept 1966
Child of Nadine Folckomer and John Haskett
Amanda Irene b. 31 Aug 1991
Bradley Charles
b.25 July 1970
Gregory Alan
b. 2 Mar 1972

Children of Karen Siggelkow and Edward Bernier
Sherri Kay   =   Daemon Alexander Lucien
b.16 Apr 1968   b. 25 Apr 1968
       m. 30 Dec 1995
       Children of Sherri Bernier and Daemon Lucien:
       Jeremy Xavier Bernier-Lucien (Remy) b. 1 Oct 1998
       Christopher Alexander Bernier-Lucien b. 20 Dec 2005
Janice Marie
b.30 Oct 1970
       Child of Janice Bernier:
       Emily Grace b. 6 Feb 2006

Printed in the United States
By Bookmasters